BOLOS &
BARISHYNAS

*Being an account of the doings of the
Sadleir-Jackson Brigade, and Altham
Flotilla, on the North Dvina during
the Summer, 1919*

The Naval & Military Press Ltd

❖

Reproduced by kind permission of the Central Library,
Royal Military Academy, Sandhurst

Published by

The Naval & Military Press Ltd

Unit 10, Ridgewood Industrial Park,

Uckfield, East Sussex,

TN22 5QE England

Tel: +44 (0) 1825 749494

Fax: +44 (0) 1825 765701

www.naval-military-press.com

© The Naval & Military Press Ltd 2004

In reprinting in facsimile from the original, any imperfections are inevitably reproduced and the quality may fall short of modern type and cartographic standards.

AT TROITSA.

Part of the Flotilla (from left to right):—H.M. M.31; H.M. R.Bs. 1 and 2;
Hospital Carrier; H.M.S. "Hyderabad"; H.M. M.27; and H.M. S.B. 1.

On Sentry at midnight.

The Balloon of amazing fecundity, with four of her offspring.

A FOREWORD

For all the sins of omission and commission that this little book reveals I crave forgiveness. With the materials that came to my hand I have endeavoured to weave a chronicle of the events that occurred on the Dvina in the memorable summer of 1919. I proffer my sincerest thanks to all those officers and men who produced the narratives, without which it would have been impossible to write this history.

To General L. de V. Sadleir-Jackson, C.B., C.M.G., D.S.O., Captain Edward Altham, C.B., R.N., Colonel H. H. Jenkins, C.M.G., D.S.O., Colonel C. S. Davies, C.M.G., D.S.O., Major A. E. Percival, D.S.O., M.C., and Captain S. F. Pickering, I am especially indebted for their valuable help and guidance.

To the Editor of *Blackwood's Magazine* I am particularly grateful for permission to take extracts from "The Little Adventure."

If this little book succeeds, as I hope it will, in reviving the memory of the Dvina days to those who served in North Russia, then indeed I shall feel that my work has not been in vain.

G. R. SINGLETON-GATES.

London,
April, 1920.

CONTENTS

LIST OF ILLUSTRATIONS

BOLOS AND BARISHYNAS

CHAPTER I

HOW WE WENT TO RUSSIA.

PARK ROYAL, N.W. Empty huts, deserted parade grounds, overgrown lawns, occasional daffodils. There, in the April sunshine and showers of peace year, the Russian Relief Force was born.

Imagine the stupendous and inspiring drama of the year of tragedy, 1914, re-staged in miniature.

The setting and the costumes are the same. The same crowds invade the deserted camp. Out from the obscurity of the streets of the cities and the lanes of freshening country they come to this camp, set in a suburb of London. From all borders, all counties, all shires they come, strange in their dialects, strange in their garb, strange in their first shyness. They hide, as the race ever does, emotion and feeling.

Just a handful at first—perhaps twenty or thirty ; but behind and around them one sees the ghosts of the far-away days of early war. They materialize in one's vision. The arts, the professions, the trades, each pouring out its torrent of men, marching awkwardly, solemnly, clad in every variety of civilian clothing.

1

Then, with a tremor and the queerest of pulsations
in the throat, one realizes the years that lie between.
The mind steals back to the fateful days that marked
for most the opening of the Great Adventure. One
remembers those familiar battlefields—Ypres, Festu-
bert, High Wood, Thiepval, Cambrai—on which that
drama was played out and where lie its actors.

These are the ghosts of the men who have passed—
the men whose splendid virility, whose promise of
fruitful manhood lies in the bosom of France.

And it is here, in their silent and invisible presence
that the curtain rises on another drama.

Who are these men ? Perhaps to the outsiders'
eye they look much the same as the men of 1914.
They are still in mufti. Worn clothes, jackets in
which the pockets droop pitiably, collars devoid of
all ties, ties to which no collars give effect, baggy
trousers, boots thin and cracked. Derby hats of pre-
war vintage, caps of faded hues, even the " decayed
Homburg hat "—five years older and sensibly more
decayed. They still look anything but soldiers.

But there is a strangely perceptible difference. For
shoulders are straighter and broader, heads more
erect, an absence of slouching.

> " For 'e saw the set o' my shoulders,
>   An' I couldn't 'elp 'olding straight,
>   When me and the other rookies
>   Come under the barrick gate."

And in their eyes there is a look—a little of
hardness, a little of fatalism and much of humour—

the things that distinguish, to those who observe, the man who went from the man who did not.

Why are they here? What is it in the past that calls them back—in the memories of shell-swept roads at night, with hurrying, silent men and rattling limbers—in the desolation of mud and wire seen from some post by the cold light of flares—of the flies that rise from some deserted trench as one walks down it— of the scream and crash of the barrage—of red, gaping, ghastly wounds and of Death.

What seek these men? Is it the spirit of adventure, dominant above all else? Is it humanitarianism that leads them to succour a nation in distress? Is it that they have probed the mirage of civilian life, and, buffeted and bruised, they drift back to the old familiar things?

Only the inmost heart of the man can answer these questions.

They are a motley crew. Here a late Major, with the Distinguished Service Order; he commanded a battery of field guns at Ypres in 1917. There an ex-Captain of Lovat's Scouts, with the Military Cross and the Mons Star; a late R.F.C. pilot; many subalterns; ex-sergeant-majors, with Distinguished Conduct Medals; quartermaster-sergeants; corporals— but private soldiers all.

*   *   *   *   *

The natural question that arises is, why such an expedition to North Russia was necessary or expedient. The amazing events of the closing months of 1918—the downfall of German power, the armistice, the Peace Conference—sufficed completely to occupy the public mind, and few, if any, remembered that in far-away Russia a handful of British troops had, since May, 1918, kept Germany from acquiring and utilizing the Murmansk Coast as a submarine base; and, further and far more important, had arrested the flow of German troops to the Western Front at a most critical juncture—namely, the conclusion of the German offensive in the spring. From September, 1917, German divisions had been transferred from Russia to France and Belgium at an average rate of six per month. But from the moment British troops landed, in June to September, when the tide in France had turned and the Germans were obliged, in spite of all risks, to send reinforcements westward, not a single German division was withdrawn from Russia. During this period Hindenburg asked urgently for ten divisions to be sent to him from this theatre, only to be told that not one could be spared. The Germans could not face the risk of a popular Russian rising.

The further query then arises as to why that British force was not withdrawn after the signing of the armistice in November, 1918. In the first instance, the port of Archangel was freezing up. In the second, the internal situation in Russia demanded the continuance of such a force in the north. An Allied front protected the inhabitants of North Russia from the spreading ravages of Bolshevism—an era of savagery of which atrocities such as these are typical :—

  "In a property near Gomel, Bolsheviks broke into a house where a mother and her four children were dining ; they cut off the mother's head and threw it in the soup tureen ; then the children's, one of which they put on each plate."

" The prisoners taken out to Machouk were made to dig their own graves, and buried alive. Axes were used to drive back into their living tomb any who tried to escape."

No one—least of all a nation which so recently engaged herself for a broken word—could abandon a helpless people to such a fate.

Early, then, in 1919 the existence of a force in North Russia was brought vividly to the realization of the British public by the medium of the daily Press. General Ironside, commanding at Archangel, indicated in messages to the War Office, that the Bolshevik forces opposing him were contemplating offensive action, with a view to acquiring the North Russian territory, thus far intact from their devastating influence. Help was needed. Reinforcements and relief were two essentials for tired, worn-out men. Finally the announcement of the formation of a Russian Relief Force was made public. Officers and men, serving and demobilized, poured into the War Office and Scotland Yard, proffering their services in any capacity. Thus the Russian Relief Force came into being.

Its task was primarily to relieve the men who had endured the rigours of the Arctic winter. But there was a far greater, a far more inspiring task ahead. The people of North Russia living under our protection were every day gaining courage and heart, and every day showed an increase of recruits to the Russian Army which was in the process of formation by the local governments under the direction of General Ironside at Archangel and General Maynard at Murmansk. British troops at these ports were training and equipping these recruits, and turning them into complete units. But in this connection it must be remembered that it is the influence and example of British grit and character that tells with all foreigners, and this was the chief factor in heartening the Russians to stand alone. It was estimated that in three or four months the Russian forces would be able to take the field by themselves. Then and then only could the British troops withdraw.

Officers and men alike, once at Park Royal, became impatient. They chafed at the delay of equipping the force, the hesitancy, the vagueness of the expedition, the lack of knowledge of the actual situation, the ignorance of prevailing conditions. An unreasonable attitude, possibly. But, having volunteered to go to Russia, they wanted to go—at once. Equipping proceeded. A civilian brigade became a brigade khakied and be-ribboned.

The wave of restlessness grew stronger. Men grew tired of waiting, and when allowed on leave failed to return. The roll of absentees grew.

The last week of April brought news of a projected move to Sandling camp in Kent, and finally the Brigade left Park Royal behind and settled in Sandling.

More equipping, efforts at training, all the necessary and essential precautions and preparations for service.

All the fearsome inoculations for typhoid and cholera, the rigours of gas chambers, the reawakening of the spirit of discipline dormant in these men.

Finally, that last inspection and the presentation of colours by General Lord Henry Rawlinson on the 22nd day of May. Then the amazing change of a month became manifest. This was no brigade of recruits. All the units were of the same character. Tanned by the sun, hardened by service abroad, officers and men alike left no doubt as to their efficiency.

A few days later, on the 27th and the last day of May, the force left the sun-kissed county of Kent.

Over the ridge at Sandling came the morning sun, catching the gorse and broom in a blaze of gold. Down the long, stony tracks from the camps poured marching bodies of laughing, jesting men, rifles over one arm, kit-bags under the other, to the tune " Good by—ee : Don't sigh—ee," heard how many times on the roads of France.

A station thronged with troops—a worried Railway Transport Officer—a harassed station-master—a few canteen workers—officers organizing entrainment.

Then a few shouted good-byes—a whistle—the train moves—a mighty cheer of joy, and we are *en route*.

And so to Newcastle and Tilbury Dock, where the majority of the absentees suddenly appear. Two more arrive in what is apparently their private tugboat, when the ship is already under weigh, while the third and last—missing for some three weeks—is not dis-covered until the following morning, when he is found playing in his accustomed place in the band.

The Brigade at the period of embarkation was under the command of Brigadier-General L. W. de Vere Sadleir-Jackson, C.B., C.M.G., D.S.O. Infantry was represented by two Service Battalions of the Royal Fusiliers, the 45th and the 46th Battalions, commanded respectively by Lieutenant-Colonel C. S. Davies, D.S.O., of the Leicestershire Regiment, and Lieutenant-Colonel H. H. Jenkins, D.S.O., of the South African Infantry ; and the 201st Battalion of the Machine Gun Corps, commanded by Lieutenant-Colonel R. J. Clark, C.M.G., D.S.O.

The other units in this force were the 55th Battery R.F.A. (Captain G. P. Simpson, M.C., R.F.A.) ; the 250th Signal Company R.E. (Captain W. B. Wishaw, M.C., R.E.) ; and the 385th Field Company R.E. (Major H. Luby, D.S.O., M.C., R.E.).

The Brigade embarked at various ports—Leith, Newcastle, and Tilbury—in the course of the final week of May and the first week of June.

*   *   *   *   *

On shipboard all ideas, conversations, actions, run in the deepest of grooves—even on a transport. But, then, all voyages were ever the same. Ulysses, one feels sure, drank gin in the smoke-room and joined in the sweep on the day's run—and then, no doubt, tampered, to his own ends, with the patent log.

After all the parades that the Army inexorably demands shall be performed between sunrise and noonday there come the gathering of little groups, discussing, in the lounge, on deck, the Derby, the day's run, the midnight sun, mines, the chances of rough weather.

Photo : Elliott & Fry]　　　　　　　　　　　　　[London, W.

GENERAL L. de V. SADLEIR-JACKSON,
C.B., C.M.G., D.S.O.,

Who commanded the Brigade of his name on the Dvina.

The laughter of men comes up from the forewell deck. In a ring of men two Marines engage in a rough-and-tumble. Two Irishmen spar with the gloves. The intensely critical spectators advise, remonstrate, cheer and laugh. Their plaudits urge the combatants to Trojan efforts.

Crack-kk-kk-kk-kk. From the stern comes the vicious rattle of a Lewis gun. Packing cases make wonderful targets at sea. But the shooting is too good. They last but a few seconds, and then are shattered to become the flotsam and jetsam of the restless waters.

The dinner bugle goes. There is a rush on deck, a falling in of men in orderly ranks. In an instant the men disappear and the decks are silent and deserted, save for an occasional sentry pacing to and fro, or an orderly officer going to or coming from duties.

Divine service on a foggy Sunday morning. A short sermon from the Senior Chaplain. " The sea is His and He made it." A raucous " Hear, hear " from the ship's siren. Sirens are most understanding instruments. " But the enemy has held it for four years," goes on the reverend.

The siren shrieks twice in spirited protest. The representative of H.M. Navy on board looks quizzically at the speaker, and turns his eyes seaward with a smile. Then the ending, " Now to God the Father ——"

More blasts from the siren, drowning for an instant the sound of men's voices raised in hymnal praise— then a hushed silence—a blessing—the hymn for His

B

Majesty—sharp words of command—quick movements of men.

Divine Service is over.

Murmansk, mirages, and the midnight sun. Seven days at sea, and the convoy anchors in the harbour of the quaint northern port, under the stern of H.M.S. *Glory*, with the seaplane carriers *Pegasus* and *Nairana* and the hospital ship *Garth Castle* as company. And overhead swings an observation balloon, a reminder of less pleasant days in another area of war. Fears of the proximity of a front are dispelled by the intimation that it is only a wireless balloon.

The photographic record of this expedition should be, if ever compiled, a most comprehensive one. After four years of prohibition, cameras are coming into their own. Whereby the midnight sun must assuredly be growing in lustre from pardonable pride. Never has he been so vehemently discussed or so ardently photographed. Later the interest in the sun is temporarily diverted by mirages of snow-covered cliffs and inverted fishing smacks. But the sun is ever first favourite.

Early next morning up anchor, out from the harbour, and away. The temperature drops when we enter the White Sea. Ice is sighted, and the vessels pass through a fast-melting ice-floe. Eleven days out, and on the morning of the twelfth we wake to view the white walls, red roofs, and green and gold minarets of Archangel.

*　　　*　　　*　　　*　　　*

Archangel was depressingly uninteresting. Even the presence of G.H.Q., in all its attendant glory, surrounded by satellites in the shape of American, French, Italian, and Russian Headquarters, failed to stir us to enthusiasm.

Our arrival almost affected Russian impassivity. A most elaborate ceremony awaited us. Under the shadow of the great white cathedral, the infantry battalions of the Brigade marched past the Russian authorities, while the Brigadier received bread and salt and an address of welcome. It was all very splendid, and our first impressions of Russian troops were appreciative of their bearing and their qualities. Alas! we were the more deceived. A final greeting from the civilian White Guard, and we marched away through the strangely primitive streets to our barracks.

But the private soldier was not yet at home in Russia. His comparatively wonderful French failed him completely. *Combien* merely produced a more pronounced vacuity in the face of the Russian vendor. Though after twenty-four hours everyone knew the utility of *kharasho* (all right) and *dobra* (good) ; and the old familiar " finish " became a potent factor in conversation.

Dull as the base proved to be, there was some little enlivenment, due to rumour. Bases were ever beset by rumour, and North Russia was no exception. The Bolsheviks were in flight, or they were advancing on Archangel in seven-league boots ; or the Germans had refused to sign the Peace terms, and hostilities had reopened ; or we were to be recalled to England at once, or we were to expect no mails. They were all pure fantasies, but as basic facts for vehement argument in the Mess they were invaluable.

One Major of the 46th wanted to dash up country at once. After three days of Archangel so did everyone else. The Major had heard that the skies were black with duck, and the lakes boiled with fish whose penchant for dry fly surpassed that of any known piscatorial variety. As he is amazingly expert at casting, and his snipe record is known throughout India, this restlessness on his part caused us no surprise. We all had guns and rods. Valises of enormous proportions contained more sporting accoutrements than those needed for the prosecution of war. The potentialities of trout breakfasts and duck dinners, viewed from the base, were enormous. What developed must be revealed later.

At least, we had our river houseboat party in Peace year. Admittedly space was limited and luxury at a minimum. When a battalion of officers and men, in addition to rations for fourteen days, occupies one barge, surplus room is quite unknown. So for over 200 miles of the Dvina the whole Brigade fed the Russian mosquito as that insect had never before been fed. A mighty ukase must have gone forth to all mosquito tribes in North Russia, for the pestilent brutes attended the barges in their tens of thousands. Patent remedies and deterrents merely acted as choice cocktails. In desperation one man appealed to a Medical Officer to be completely painted with iodine. The Medical Officer sympathetically pointed out that transport facilities were extremely limited, and the

War Office, though indulgent to a degree, could hardly
be expected to allow innumerable general service
wagons, loaded with iodine tubes, to follow the column.
So, with calm resignation, the man went back to his
bitten fate.

One of the advantages of twenty-four hours of daylight rested in the fact that it seemed no imposition
to stop at two o'clock in the morning and order the
Brigade to bathe and breakfast. The Russian peasant
in the villages along the river always seemed to be
awake, no matter the hour. Bearded old men, in
faded red and blue blouses, would shyly gather and
quizzically regard the troops. Their womenfolk, much
less shy, would barter eggs and milk for our staple
diet of beef and biscuit. Butter we purchased at six
shillings a pound. One spirited Mess President even
produced cream cheese.

On the evening of June 21st a sports meeting was
organized on shore, and during a strenuous bout of
" wrestling on horseback " a sapper of the Field
Company had the misfortune to fall and fracture one
of his legs. First aid was rendered as efficiently as the
skill and means available would allow, and the patient
was taken back on to the R.E. barge. At this juncture
a large paddle steamer was observed approaching,
so the unfortunate man was hustled into the tug, with
a small party under an officer, in an attempt to inter-
cept the new vessel. Attempts to stop the elegant
steamer were frustrated at first. Finally, the tug
persistently lay in the other vessel's course, and the
latter came to a stop.

The officer discovered then, to his astonishment and alarm, that he had held up the G.H.Q. ship *Retvizan*, carrying the Commander-in-Chief and his staff. The injured man had the time of his life during his journey to Archangel on board her.

A solemn *storasta* (headman) of one village conducted a battalion headquarters in state to his log cabin, to the intense approval of his three daughters and the serious diminution of his stores of tea. The Russian's capacity for tea from a samovar is colossal. Everyone aimed at being truly polite, but the strain of imbibing gallons of tea was enormous. Nothing was more welcome than the warning of the tug's siren.

For five days and nights the barges moved slowly up the Dvina. The thrilling prospect of a Bolshevik demonstration from the wooded banks was never realized. In this amazing war, with a line of communication of 800 miles, that danger was always imminent. But either the Bolshevik had departed from our flank or we had awed him completely. First contact with the enemy was after we had disembarked at Bereznik and Ossinova, the advanced bases. Three scouts, complete with the latest information regarding the Bolsheviks, were captured at G.H.Q. At Bereznik the Brigade was joined by a Russian battalion— " Dyer's Battalion," of not inconsiderable fame. And not only men, but women also. The Commanding Officer, Royal Engineers, had among his sappers several sturdy ex-Bolshevik women, and as Royal Engineers they were quite useful. Striking evidence of the adaptability of the Russian was shown when a party of Bolo prisoners arrived at the advanced cage. One of their number volunteered to guard them. He was given a British forage cap, a rifle and small-arm ammunition, and he proceeded to his duty with perfect sangfroid. Admittedly, the late Bolsheviks were enjoying what was probably their most substantial meal for a fortnight; yet the Gilbertian aspect of the situation remained. Later the guard and the guarded fought in our Russian battalions against the Bolo.

Our arrival at Bereznik coincided with the departure from the shores of Russia of the troops we had come to relieve. It is well that the story of their endurance has been made known. They have left behind their quota of brave British hearts, and the Russian will tend their resting-places.

It was at Bereznik also that the fame of the angling Major spread throughout the land. By virtue of much skill in casting an " orange quill " upon the waters, the mess breakfasted daily on a variety of roach, a delectable change from salt bacon. The catch one morning was twenty-nine, and the Major, though thoroughly soaked to the waist, was radiantly happy.

The next afternoon in the orderly-room the Adjutant was aroused from his slumbers by a violent ringing of the telephone.

" G.H.Q. to speak to Major Nightingale."

It was regretted that he was not in camp.

" Would you send for him immediately, please, for the Commander-in-Chief ?"

Runners dashed hither and thither to discover an

officer who had so suddenly leapt into prominence. In due course the Major arrived.

"The C.-in-C.'s compliments to Major Nightingale, and where does he get his fish ?"

"In a lake beyond the village of Ossinova, sir."

"Could we have a more definite location, please ?"

It was given.

Then : "And what is the time to fish ?"

"Oh ! the General should come down between the hours of twelve and three in the morning, sir."

"Thank you." Br-rr-rr.

The General never appeared at the lake to fish with the commando, though they looked expectantly for him in the grey dawn of every morning.

Encouraged by our arrival, strengthened by our presence, raised in moral by our enthusiasm, the loyal Russian troops in the forward zone, led into attack by British officers, captured two villages of considerable importance, Troitsa and Topsa. The Bolshevik suffered somewhat, for he lost several commissars, including the chief of the Archangel district.

Our own force, not yet wanted for action, continued training and idling in the warm July sunshine, when suddenly we were plunged into stark tragedy. Mutiny, butchery, the horror of revolution of the primitive, raged among us. Russian troops, comprising "Dyer's Battalion," upon whom so much careful work and energy had been expended, and in whom we had all such pregnant hopes, rose and foully butchered their British and Russian officers, roamed through Topsa and Troitsa, blazing indiscriminately with Lewis guns

and rifles, and then a wild revolutionary rabble, disorganized and awed by a few cool, steady British soldiery, fled into the woods and joined the Bolsheviks.

The daily Press of England has contained in its
columns so many misleading statements, so many false
conclusions with reference to this mutiny, that a short
retrospection into the formation of " Dyer's Battalion "
is necessary.

Bolshevik prisoners and deserters, secured during
the winter months, had been incarcerated at Archangel. Composed almost entirely of peasantry, these
men had been mobilized by the Bolshevik forces,
driven into an army of communists, and commissars,
forced to fight under the threat of instant death and
reprisals on their women and children, yet, withal,
held together from very fear. Their clothing was
poor, their rations of bread and dried fish totally inadequate. To these simple fearing peasantry came
strange rumours of good food, warm clothing prevalent
in the ranks of their enemies. They were warned often
of the " Anglo-French and Japanese American robbers
and executioners."*

Nevertheless, many of them came over to our lines,
or were captured in minor operations throughout the
long winter. By dint of reasonable treatment and
propaganda, there followed the inevitable reaction
against the Bolshevik creed. Their numbers were
sufficient to justify the proposal that they should be
turned into an armed force to support our weak forces

* I quote from an official order of the 6th Bolshevik army.
dated the 30th October, 1918.

against their late compatriots. This was actually done, and the 1st Battalion of the Slavo-British Legion came into being.

The difficulty that existed at that time, and existed, indeed, throughout all our work in North Russia, was the question of the officer. So very few of the old Tzarist army officers had escaped to the northern anti-Bolshevik forces during the tragic months of revolution. All that had so escaped were serving with loyal Russian troops. In officering the S.B.L., there were two alternatives before the General Commanding—either to have all British officers, or else create officers from the shopkeeper and working class of Archangel. The former plan was impossible, owing to the dearth of such officers. The latter, therefore, came into operation, and, in addition, a few British officers, some of the most able in the country, were attached to the regiment to shape its destiny.

Unhappily, the Russian officer, in commanding men, uses methods of a different character to our own. They are harsh and tyrannical, using blows to enforce obedience ; but, what is worse, they have no conception of devoting themselves to the interests of their men, feeding them, clothing them, ministering to their welfare and comfort—attentions which bring their reward in loyalty and devotion. On the contrary, these officers, given power, authority, privileges, think of nothing else. To exert these powers, to drink and be merry, constitutes the day. The men must look after themselves.

Thus, Bolshevik agents, introduced in the S.B.L.,

having full scope, spread their insidious doctrines, reawakening the ideas that these ignorant peasantry had put aside. No one suspected such a movement. The native officers, who might have been cognizant of the sowing of the seeds of revolt, were idling. They had no interest in their men, in their thoughts or their actions. The plans for mutiny, organized by an agent who held the rank of sergeant, matured. And on the morning of July 7th, as the sun rose, five British officers were attacked in their billets and riddled with bullets and rent with bayonets.

On board H.M.S. *Humber*, lying in mid-stream, the sound of firing was thought to be someone trying a machine gun, but as the noise persisted it became evident that something in the nature of a " scrap " was taking place in the village, and possibly that the Bolos had sprung a sudden attack on the troops.

At about 3.30 a.m. a man came down on the beach abreast the ship and began to walk into the river shouting for help.

From a distance he appeared to be dressed in a dull blue suit with a large red stripe down the left side. It was thought he must be an escaped Bolo prisoner.

A boat was sent over to him, and he was then heard to shout, " For God's sake, send a boat ; I am shot ! "

The boat picked him up and took him on board the *Humber*, and the doctor saw and attended to him, and it was discovered that he was a Captain Barr, who was attached to this so-called " Loyal " Russian regiment.

He reported that his men had mutinied and shot

their officers. Captain Barr was found to have many bullet-holes in various parts of his body, and it was estimated that he had been shot ten times. He was dressed in blue pyjamas, and the red stripe proved to be blood from a wound in the chest.

He had walked about two miles in this state, and was thoroughly exhausted.

Lieutenant-Commander A. Johnstone, R.N., of the *Humber*, relating the incident, said that to the ship's company Captain Barr was a perfect marvel, in that he had survived this horrible shooting, that he had walked all that distance in the state in which he was found, and for the wonderful stamina and pluck with which he must have been imbued.

" We all felt that he was one in a thousand, and it was with great regret that we heard of his death, some days afterwards, as he was being put on board a hospital carrier at Archangel after a journey of 200 miles down river—a journey which must have been a severe test for anyone, even slightly wounded.

" An attempt to describe our feelings of admiration for this very gallant gentleman could only give a poor idea of what those feelings were."

During the hours of turmoil Troitsa was a most unpleasant spot. Various elements of Brigade headquarters had moved up river, and at the moment of disturbance were peacefully asleep in what is now known as Mutiny Village. The noise of the firing of rifles awoke Major Straker, Chief Intelligence Officer, and Captain Pickering, Staff Captain. A momentary glance from the windows revealed a few Russians

strolling aimlessly about in the grey light of dawn.
There being no accounting for what a Russian soldier
may or may not do, the awakened pair retired to
rest.

A continuance of the shooting and much shouting
occasioned another rising. Straker and Pickering
donned gum boots and British warms, awakened the
remainder, and departed to discover the *raison d'être*
of these alarming sounds of battle.

" Q " Department, represented by a voluble Australian Major, was visibly annoyed at being disturbed.
He pointed out with considerable vehemence that
mutinies came entirely under " G." " What the
hell has it to do with ' Q ' and who the devil
woke me up ?"

The unheeding companions of the Major searched
in a frenzy in the half light for revolvers and boots.
There was a universal shortage of revolver ammunition,
and recriminations became more bitter and the search
for it more frenzied as the firing and the shouting grew
more intense.

Meanwhile Straker and Pickering, having reached
the street, called at the hospital fifty yards away,
seeking information. They discovered a Russian
medical officer, prostrate with fear and completely
ignorant of the reasons of the tumult. As the pair
emerged from the hospital, a horde of shrieking,
mutinous troops from " Dyer's Battalion " surged round
them, menacing them with revolvers, bayonets, and
even Lewis guns. The complete absence of weapons
on Straker and Pickering undoubtedly saved their

lives at this critical juncture. Discretion bade them yield to the mutineers, and wisely they did so.

The last seen of them for some considerable time was their exit from the village, completely surrounded by the howling mob. The obvious intention of the Russians was to lead them to execution. Why they hesitated will always be a mystery, for their epithets were hardly of the nature to elevate the hopes of our two heroes. What actually happened was that the pair were incarcerated in a bath house, under guard of two sentries with Lewis guns, one engaging the door, the other the window.

Alternatives for escape were eagerly discussed. Major Straker, with much glee, produced an army pattern knife and proposed to stab the sentry on duty at the window. The other sentry would then, naturally, enter the door, upon which his head would be beaten in by Pickering with an earthenware pail—the sole toilet utensil of the bathroom. The drill of this was rehearsed, but, unfortunately, the window sentry was just beyond the reach of Straker's arm. The door suddenly opened. The dread moment had come. They were going out to die! No; it was merely another pair of captives—Colonel Lowrie, of the Marines, and a newspaper correspondent. The door closed again. The council of war was now augmented, and further deliberations as to the possibility of escape took place.

The shriek of an approaching shell caused a cessation of talk. The burst was a hundred yards away. This complication of matters was far from aiding the calm consideration of plans for gaining freedom. Another arrived. The splinters could be heard tearing into the logs of the hut. The third shell tactfully removed the roof of the bath-house, smothering the assembled prisoners with debris.

The guard, resentful of this unreasonable treatment, departed at a furious pace, and from the damaged bath-house emerged four free men.

The experience of those who had remained in the billet was hardly so harrowing. Bullets tore through the woodwork and windows, resulting in everyone conforming as much as possible to the floor.

The C.R.E., of monumental proportions, caused some apprehension by his inability to entirely reduce himself below the level of the window.

The sudden arrival of Straker and Pickering cheered the beleaguered enormously. A few more shells came over, and then the noise died away.

The danger was over. The shelling from the guns at Topsa had commenced the rout of the mutineers. How and why those particular shells arrived when they did was only revealed later. General Grogan, in his pyjamas, when the outbreak commenced, had made a reconnaissance of Troitsa, and, finding it in the hands of the mutineers, decided to shell the village.

A Russian battery was at the time billeted close by, and, as was only to be expected, they joined, not in the mutiny, but in the general pandemonium of firing. With the aid of the C.R.A. (Major Burdon), an attempt was made by the General to shell Troitsa. No one could interpret his wishes to the Russian battery commander, owing to ignorance of the language. This commander, moreover, had very strong views of his own as to the best spot at which to fire. Resultantly the shells went well over the village. Finding gesticulation a failure, the C.R.A. pulled the gunner aside and laid the gun on a house in Troitsa. Signs to the gunner to fire appeared to be understood. Whereupon he proceeded to turn the handles, and pointed the gun elsewhere, expressing his opinions in voluble Russian.

The C.R.A. again interfered, relaid the gun, and the pantomime was repeated. So it continued till the Russian Brigadier arrived. He awed the gunners, and finally, to their chagrin and the cheers of the assembled British staff, the first shell departed on its way to the village of Troitsa.

The effect of this shelling was immediate. Mutineers dispersed in every direction. Hastily organized bodies of signallers and the Royal Army Service Corps assisted in the pursuit. The Navy then arrived in the form of a landing party from H.M. Monitor 31. Those scoundrels who escaped capture fled to the woods.

The news of the outbreak reached Brigade Head-quarters at Ossinova by wireless, with a request for troops to be sent up. Colonel Jenkins, with " C " Company (Captain Blackburn, M.C.) and the Head-quarters Company of the 46th Royal Fusiliers, were embarked with rations, stores, and vast quantities of small-arm ammunition on board the river steamer *Retvizan*, at that time, in use by the Commander-in-Chief.

AT ARCHANGEL.

General Sadleir-Jackson receiving an Address of Welcome from the Civil Authorities at Archangel on the Arrival of the Brigade. General Ironside, the Commander-in-Chief, is standing to the right rear of General Jackson.

UP THE DVINA.

How we proceeded up the mighty Dvina from the Base. Note the Men on the Roof of the Barge and the Pile of Wood Fuel in the Stern of the Tug.

General Ironside, looking worried and not a little
sad, journeyed with the troops. A five hours' run, and
Troitsa was reached.

Calm had been restored some considerable time,
but the reinforcements were welcome, especially as
the Bolshevik himself was becoming particularly
active.

The landing parties of sailors and marines, who had
formed a line of defence, were the greatest hosts imaginable. The sailor loves to go ashore for a " scrap,"
but he does like particularly to mix up with the
soldier men

Eventually the line was consolidated, and fears of
another outbreak were dispersed by the disarming of
all Russian troops ; and a telegram was dispatched to
Bahkaritza, near Archangel, to disarm a second battalion in training there. The ex-Bolos were subsequently turned into labour companies.

In such wise was the patient work of a winter
completely and utterly destroyed. In their inmost
hearts the loyal Russians were not sorry. They
regretted the butchery of British officers, but the
mutiny itself they regarded as the natural and inevitable outcome of the whole effort. They merely
shrugged their shoulders as if to say, " We told
you so."

From such officers and men as these General Ironside
with indefatigable patience and forbearance, tried to
create a fighting unit. He failed, and the Russians
sneered. Possibly posterity in North Russia, if it is
ever civilized sufficiently, will recognize that effort as

c

an heroic attempt by a gallant gentleman to make a people save themselves. For such it was.

The Bolshevik, at times capable of considerable foresight, made the most of the mutiny, which he had himself engineered. He attacked with a show of force on the Troitsa bank (the right bank) of the Dvina, and drove the Russian troops into the forest, which extended between Troitsa itself and the River Selmenga, a tributary of the Dvina. A combined British and Russian attack the next morning cleared the situation, and the Bolo retired to the far bank of the Selmenga, where he remained till the inception of the crushing defeat he received in August.

The remaining companies of the 46th Battalion Royal Fusiliers and the 45th Battalion Royal Fusiliers arrived in the next few days. The latter battalion took over the defence of the left bank, while the former remained on the Troitsa (right) bank. Journeying up river was a dreadful concern, and entailed much travail in loading and unloading barges, owing to the complete absence of piers capable of having barges moored alongside.

The chief trial in moving units was the question of baggage. Before the Brigade left England, gum boots thigh had been issued in bulk. Each battalion had over a thousand in huge packing cases, and whithersoever the battalions went the gum boots thigh went with them. The men grew to loathe the very mention of gum boots thigh. The Quartermasters dreaded to examine a case, for fear of seeing one of the accursed things. We had been led to expect great swamps.

There may have been in the spring ; but as the summer was tropical, the swamps had disappeared. The gum boots thigh, however, remained. They were a pestilence and a plague among us. Humbly we begged to be allowed to return them to Ordnance. But the reluctance of that department to issue what is necessary is as nothing to its unwillingness to receive back into its fold all superfluous things.

The men therefore continued to suffer from aching backs, and the Quartermasters grew more and more morose. Finally the strain grew intolerable. We sailed away one afternoon, and left our thousands of gum boots behind us on the Dvina beach. Backs became straight, and the Quartermasters praised the High Gods on Olympus, who control the destinies of army dumps.

How some of the unit's transport came by road is a story worth telling. The case of the Engineers is a typical one. On receipt of orders to move to Troitsa by road, the company was at Bereznik. Stores and kits were packed and sorted out, the absolute minimum being put aside to accompany the unit by road, the remainder being destined to remain behind and come up by barge later.

On July 5th ponies and Russian country carts were drawn from the A.S.C., and such stores as were to accompany the column loaded up. Of the country carts much might be said. Heath-Robinson, in his wildest flights of imagination, never pictured such memorials of dilapidation. One collapsed completely shortly after leaving the A.S.C. lines, and of the remainder not one possessed a complete tyre.

What did duty therefore usually consisted of a few bent pieces of very corroded hoop-iron attached to the rim or felloe by string. The felloe, in the majority of cases, had pieces 10 to 12 inches in length missing therefrom, the gap being bridged by the aforesaid hoop-iron, the whole providing a very excellent example of interdependability. The several pieces of metal doing duty as a tyre depended entirely upon the felloe to complete the gaps therein and maintain it roughly—very roughly—in circular form, while the several pieces of timber constituting the felloe relied entirely upon the tyre to perform a like service for them, the whole being entirely dependent on the string to maintain any form of connection between it and the spokes. However, the worst of the carts were patched up as well as the time and circumstances permitted, and by late afternoon the column moved off on its journey to Troitsa.

For the first 15 versts or thereabouts the journey was along a sandy track through the forest, and here transport difficulties really commenced. The sand was so loose that the carts, all overladen, sank almost to the axles, and as each was drawn by one Russian pony progress was slow and difficult, and in many places had to be assisted by parties of sappers. About midnight the column entered a large clearing in the forest, the track here crossing a deep ravine down which the carts, with wheels " spragged," had to be handled one at a time and man-handled up the other side, during which they usually shed all or part of their loads. Eventually the ravine was crossed and the column moved on, arriving at Priluk about 1.30 a.m. on July 6th, the last hour of the march being done in pouring rain. At Priluk billets were obtained, and within half an hour of arrival everyone had settled down to obtain such sleep as mosquitoes and other members of the insect world, which abound in Russian houses, permitted.

Later in the morning the weather cleared and afforded a much-desired opportunity for drying boots and clothing, and at 3 p.m. the column moved on. The second day's journey led through many villages situated in a large cultivated clearing in the forest. During this day's trek two carts, in spite of all efforts to maintain them as a composite whole, completely disintegrated, and their loads had to be distributed over the remainder of the already over-loaded vehicles.

At about 2 a.m. on July 7th Pless was reached, where the unit billeted and later obtained good bathing. Four o'clock in the afternoon saw the march resumed, and during it the forest was re-entered, with the immediate result of the collapse of another cart. In the early hours of the 8th Kurgomin was reached. Here a signal officer existed, and for the first time since leaving Bereznik communication was obtained with Headquarters. Here, also, information was received of the mutiny of Dyer's Battalion, of the S.B.L., and of the fact that the two companies of mutineers were still at large in the forest. Tactical positions were immediately selected and the blockhouses defending Kurgomin manned.

The knowledge that six British officers had been murdered by the mutineers caused everyone to " see red," and the greatest of all hopes was that the two companies of mutineers might come within reach of Kurgomin that night. The presence of the pioneer platoon of Dyer's Battalion complicated matters somewhat, but arrangements were made to deal with any possible disturbance they might create. In justice, however, it must be said that they appeared to feel the defection of their battalion very deeply, and that they were under suspicion as a consequence thereof. There was no sign of the mutineers, however, and at 1.30 p.m. the final stage of the journey was commenced. Rain had been falling in torrents since about 10 a.m., and transport troubles increased. Shortly after leaving Kurgomin two more carts collapsed, fortunately near a village where civilian transport was requisitioned to replace them ; while shortly afterwards another two " went west." These were replaced by carts requisitioned at Topsa, and at 9 p.m. Troitsa was reached.

Relieving the Russians in the line was a strange and humorous study in psychology. The native troops spoke in hushed whispers, officers crept about like ghostly shades, and an eerie silence reigned over the line. The British soldier is easily seduced to silence in a silent land. While the Russians were actually with us in the line, we spoke in hushed whispers and crept about like ghosts.

The dawn came, and we were alone, holding the line. There must be fires, there must be wood for fires, there must be tea and bacon and fried biscuit and rum. Then the noise began. Trees were felled and came crashing down in the forest amid the cheers of the men. Raucous voices shouting for matches, insistent voices claiming bacon, the crackling of wood in the fire, sounds of chopping from every direction, soldiers alternately laughing and cursing.

The Bolshevik intelligence reports which subsequently came into our possession revealed that this period was one of considerable mystification to his commanders. They had been opposed by British before, but these British were so strange. They held gala fetes in the wood. Perhaps a celebration before battle. From that time onward nervousness that was never allayed nor stilled reigned at the Bolshevik headquarters.

At last we were at the war. A quaint war indeed, possessing little, if any, of the characteristics of the fighting in France. One novel element was the proximity and the association with the naval forces. The gunboats and the monitors, the coastal motor boats and the seaplanes, all became our very good friends. Later they served us loyally and well.

The flotilla was under command of Captain Edward Altham, C.B., R.N., whose flagship was the river steamer *Borodino*. H.M.S. *Hyderabad*, one of the " hush " ships of the war (now, alas ! sold to the shipbreakers), H.M.S. *Humber*, H.M.S. *Cicala*, and Monitors 31, 33, and 27 lay in the river near Troitsa.

Nor must one forget the Royal Air Force, under Lieutenant-Colonel Lancelot Tomkinson, with its planes on Seaplane Island, and the observation balloon of amazing fecundity. But more of that later.

The sailormen were enchanted with our brass bands. They came ashore and rode our mules, and we went abroad and distilled sweet music for them while they mixed us gin. Night on the Dvina was like a night in port when the Admiral dines in state—lights from all the vessels of war twinkling across the waters of the river, and the sound of London's music diffusing in the air. Night was never dark, but remained that strange half light in which all things seemed part of a mirage, and the harshness of material things was toned to a wonderful softness.

Naval Transport Officers and Beachmasters established themselves on the Troitsa sands. They guided the destinies of the beach with unerring precision. When work was at a minimum, they endeavoured to make the beach of pristine splendour by employing Russians to pick up stray paper.

Almost any night, between midnight and three in the morning, their slumbers were rudely disturbed by loud crashes and voluble oaths. Their tents were often in jeopardy. But the wise men in bed merely turned over, muttering curses on the Navy for dining so well at Brigade.

Life in the line during the hot scorching days of July was amusing and pleasant. Flies and mosquitoes of enormous proportions worried us a little. War itself was intensely spasmodic. When the enemy grew really nervous, the air grew thick with bullets, which tore through the tree-tops and into the bark ; but no one was ever hit. The general defensive policy of the Bolo was, upon alarm, to fire off everything and anything along his whole line, till his supply of ammunition ran short.

Occasional raids were made into his line, at which moment he would leave his dwelling with indecent haste for a safer refuge in the almost impenetrable forest. A few deserters, hungry, wretched, ill-clad, wandered into our lines. Sometimes straying sheep did the same, and strayed no more.

Bolshevik propaganda came to be circulated in some mysterious manner amongst the troops. They suggested that our men, being workers, should unite with the Russian workers, slay their officers, slay the capitalist, take control in their own hands. The men read the appeals with amusement and dismissed them with contempt. So much for this propaganda.

A dull morning gave Monitor 31 a chance for a real sensation. The vigilance of the officer of the watch resulted in the discovery of a spar floating down stream with an attached twig, to which was tied a letter The letter was hurriedly translated. The contents resulted in tremendous activity on land and water. Cipher messages and urgent priority calls disturbed the serenity of the morning. Amazing events were imminent. Liberty arose in hopefulness, stretched herself after her unconscionably long slumbering in Russia. The next morning she went to sleep again.

Nothing had happened, and nothing would happen.
So here is the letter :—

" Greetings to our dear brothers from the Red
Trenches !

" We acquaint you with the condition of the
mobilized men from the Samara region. All
mobilized and even volunteers refuse to fight for
the Commune, and the mobilized even more so.
Soon, very soon, we will bayonet our commissars
and commanders. Our comrade, the chief of the
Communists, Trotsky, has disappeared, no one
knows where. Now the game of the Communists
is played out. Soon there will be an end to the
Commune.

" Long live Liberty !

" Now, dear brothers, don't shoot at us. We
are all enemies of the Soviet rule. We are kept
in the trenches against our will, where we are
forced with whips and the threat to be shot.

" They thought to enlarge their area, but they
won't go far with the help of the mobilized, and
even the volunteers, who are against them. In the
rear the mobilized are shouting, ' Down with the
Commune ! Long live the National Assembly !'
At the aeroplanes only Communists fire.

" Long live a free Russia ! Long live the
National Assembly !

" With kind greetings to our dear brothers.
We are not your enemies, but brothers.

(Signed)   " 1st Ijinimo Pechorsky Regt."

One can understand the communists firing at the aeroplanes, for daily the villages held by the enemy behind the line were heavily bombed, with most successful results. Whenever an enemy gunboat dared to fire, she was immediately bombed by a seaplane. In some cases direct hits were obtained on gunboats by means of bombs, and the enemy fleet would decrease in size till our seaplanes showed a tendency to desist.

The Bolo fleet was commanded by an ex-bluejacket in the Russian Navy, and the officers under him were, with a few exceptions, ex-officers in the old navy, who merely served in the Red fleet to save their families from being tortured.

At times the Bolo gunboat shooting was good. But on the whole the work of the Red fleet was innocuous.

Its chief use was to provide everyone with fish from the river. A morning's bombardment by the Bolo resulted in swarms of small boats on the river—from the ships, the troops, and the villages—all gathering in the stunned pike and bream, and even salmon trout. The maidens of the hamlets (*barishynas*), in their primitive craft, were always the first to put off, and they always secured the largest fish.

Far more potent than the alarms of the Bolo were the allurements of the *barishyna*. Till the skilful hand of autumn painted the trees with russet and gold, the *barishyna* was the splendid daring splash of colour in a green and brown land.

The summer sun tanned all our faces and arms, and the limbs and feet of the women, for boots and stockings they wore only on feast days. Through the dust of the roads and the mud and slush of the tracks they walked barefoot. Yet there was never a *barishyna* bareheaded. Kerchiefs of crimson, magenta, pink, yellow and green, with brilliant markings of all these and every other colour, were bound round their heads and tied in careless knots beneath their chins.

Their clumsy bodices and skirts, faded by the scorching sunshine, retained nevertheless their early splendour of colour. Girls with bodices of green, skirts of red, and aprons of yellow, surmounted by queer brown faces, with heavy features and laughing blue eyes, passed one on the road, and smiled a greeting of the day. Loose limbed and ungainly, they walked and they worked like men. They loaded and unloaded stores from the barges at Troitsa beach. The tactful expletives of the beachmaster, in atrocious Russian, resulted in stupendous feats being accomplished by his gangs of women labourers. They handled mighty cases of rations ; they carried the huge planks for the new *preesten* (pier) : they moved great stores of ammunition, bombs and shells. And they never murmured. They worked and smiled and pondered long on the mad English, who unloaded barges and then loaded them again, who had more sugar than they could eat, and who wanted more eggs than Russian hens were capable of laying. But these young women grew to be very wise and shrewd. These English had much, therefore they could pay much. Once, in the dim early days of intervention in Russia, one tin of bully beef would produce ten eggs in exchange, a pound of sugar a chicken or vast quantities of potatoes. But the *barishynas* became profiteers. Finally one egg cost a tin of beef or half a pound of sugar, plus an hour's argument. The milk, that was once fresh and pure, they adulterated with Dvina water, and unblushingly vouched for its purity.

They drove the droskies and took rations to the line, where ofttimes their men folk would not venture. One convoy of eighteen men and two women persistently refused one morning to leave for the line. The road was heavy from sudden rains. The Bolo shelled the path intermittently. Sitting on their droskies, the male peasants refused to budge. The two women held a conference. The harassed D.A.D.S. and T., Major Watson, was contemplating the use of force, when one of the women stepped forward and jeered in voluble Russian at her cowardly male companions. She and her comrade would go for the English soldiers, even though all the others refused. The Russians, wincing beneath a woman's sneers, capitulated. Finally, led by the two Amazons, the convoy left for, and eventually arrived at, its destination.

All branches of H.M. Service that employed labour preferred women to men. They were more cheerful, more willing, and the tendency to form soviets of grousing was not so strong as with the male peasant. Certainly the women tired of work before the men, but the other compensations of willing endeavour and cheerfulness of spirit made them the more popular.

Their consciences, however, developed considerable elasticity during the campaign. In the ample folds

of their skirts and bodices they found room for tins
of condensed milk, sacks of flour and of sugar. The
latter article was their chief downfall. It was selling
among the peasants for fifty roubles (North Russian
Government rouble is equivalent to twenty-five English shillings) a pound, and when women were working
on the ration barges, the sight of sugar was always too
great a temptation for them. Their penitence on being
discovered at petty larceny was amazing. With loud
protestations and many tears, they fell upon the earth
and kissed the feet of their detector. What course is
there for a British officer in such a predicament ?
Punishment was out of the question, admonition was
restricted to the use of three or four words, and sympathy (inherent in the soldier) usually overcame the
first feelings of annoyance.

But there were moments in the campaign when
sympathy did not assume the ascendant. The execution
of the ringleaders of the mutiny in " Dyer's Battalion "
was a pitiless business. The only sadness in British
hearts was for those soldier friends who had been
killed as they slept because they chose to accept a
great trust. It was an amazing scene. Lines of
troops formed three sides of a square. They were
the remnants of "Dyer's Battalion," a battalion of
Russian infantry, and Captain Allfrey's company of
the 45th Battalion Royal Fusiliers. The fourth side
of the square was completed by twelve wooden posts.
Twelve Lewis gunners from " Dyer's Battalion " composed the firing party. Each had a gun and a drum
with five cartridges inserted.

The twelve ringleaders of the mutiny—one or two recklessly defiant, the majority broken in spirit and fearsome of death—were marched on to the parade and tied to the twelve bare wooden posts. They were blindfolded. Their sentences were read out.

The crack-kk-kk of the guns broke the tense silence. So perished those who had encompassed the deaths of gallant men who had tried to aid them, and the curtain fell on one of the greatest tragedies of the Dvina.

Certain Russian battalions at this stage in the campaign arrived, to afford our troops a short relief from the line. Drafts of officers of the Russian Army, who had been prisoners in Germany, and who had been refitted at the training camp at Newmarket, Cambridge, had lately joined these battalions.

The Colonel of one of the North Russian regiments visited the 46th Royal Fusiliers battalion headquarters.

For over two hours the general run of the line, the scheme of defence, and the method of relief, were explained to him. He expostulated and questioned till the assembled British officers grew weary. It was then after midnight. The relief should have been completed six hours before. Through his interpreter, he informed us that he was very tired. Could he rest in the village till the following day, and then proceed with the relief ?

Further argument ensued. Finally, in wearisome desperation, his wish was acceded to. Next morning before 3 a.m. the relief was cancelled, and the whole battalion was ordered across the river to the left bank.

The indefatigable N.T.O. of Troitsa was ordered to convey them across the river.

" Can you be ready in an hour ?" asked the Brigade.

" We will try. How much baggage is there ?"

" Oh, practically nothing but fighting equipment—Lewis guns and so on. They are going straight into the line," was the reply.

" Right-oh ! Send them down."

One hour later a barge lay along side the *preesten*.

Six hours later the battalion arrived on the beach from a village not three thousand yards away, with forty droskies conveying their fighting equipment.

One hour later, after tremendous effort, the whole of the battalion, plus fighting equipment, was crammed on board the barge. Tired, thirsty, pouring with perspiration and not in a particularly good temper, the wretched N.T.O. asked the Russian battalion commander if that was all.

" No, no ! The drosky with our piano has not arrived yet."

Eventually the battalion arrived on the left bank.

The Russian soldiery themselves were entirely bored with the whole proceedings. Their general attitude was one of complete disinterestedness. Yet once installed in the line, they found an urgent necessity to visit the Y.M.C.A. canteen. Less rifle or any warlike weapon, they left the line, and, unless discovered by a British soldier, remained away half a day or more.

During the closing stages of the campaign use was made of Colonel Carroll's cavalry, composed of Russian officers and men, with a British Colonel and a few

TROITSA BEACH, showing the R.A.S.C. ration barge in the foreground, the hospital, intelligence barges, the preesten, and the 201st M.G.C. camps in the background behind Troitsa Church.

British cavalry officers. There was small opportunity to test their fighting ability as cavalry, and they were used as mounted infantry. Their ponies were amazingly hardy and capable of remarkable endurance, despite the large weight carried, varying from 16 to 18 stone. The type of man was superior to the infantry. He was cleaner, possessed of slight self-respect, and with a respect for his officers.

The artillery, of which a small force served with the Brigade, was in every way superior to the other arms.

But the most untractable fellow of all was the Russian river pilot. The Dvina, towards the end of July, became abnormally low. The light fall of snow during the previous winter partly accounted for this, in conjunction with the unusually dry summer. Navigation in the channel of the river became extremely difficult. Craft aground for a few hours frequently caused the channel to alter. This entailed constant rebuoying.

The proposal to raise the height of the water in the river by means of a dam was shown to be unfeasible. The action of the river upon meeting an obstruction was to " silt up " on the down-stream side of the obstruction, and to " scour " a deep hole on the up-stream side. The result was that a fresh " bar " was created on the down-stream side, and the depth of the channel was not altered.

The unique feature of the whole of the Dvina campaign was that all stores, rations, and small-arms

D

ammunition had to be conveyed from the base to the line by this changeable river.

The numbers of light draught craft were inadequate to meet requirements, owing to large numbers having been removed the previous autumn by the enemy.

The problem of maintaining efficient communications, which had to be faced, in view of an offensive being contemplated up the Dvina River, was a considerable one. Statistics for the past twenty years showed that the river fell consistently until about August 7th, after which a rise could be expected, until the beginning of September, when a further fall would be probable. Bearing in mind the light snowfall of the previous winter, a low river was to be anticipated.

The country on both banks of the river is spruce and silver beech forests, and comes close to the water's edge ; the undergrowth is thick, but not impassable. The forests contain a great many marshes, many of which are 6 feet deep and over. In summer it may be assumed that infantry can move through the forest with difficulty. Pack animals are possible in some parts ; pack artillery and cavalry could only get through in few places. For wheeled vehicles (except country carts) the country is practically impassable.

Country carts with loads of 400 pounds could get through in places.

Villages with clearings of about 1 square mile existed along the banks of the river about every 7 versts. Speaking broadly, the peasants were apathetic as to which side occupied the villages ; if they had any feelings at all, their sympathies were pro-Bolshevik.

The Russian pilots, moreover, developed an amazing penchant for grounding barges. There was never a barge that eventually reached Troitsa that had not, during its progress up river, been aground for twelve, twenty-four, or even forty-eight hours.

The ration barge, at one period, stuck fast on the Kurgomin bar. The whole Brigade was in need of rations. Consequently all the stores on the barge had to be offloaded into small carbus barges, and then taken down to a deeper pool (Red Bank pool). Bolo prisoners, stripped naked, were used to push the carbuses from the bar into the deep water. The supplies were then loaded on to tugs and conveyed down the main channel to the forward supply depot.

The officer in charge of this particular barge had a peculiarly unpleasant time. He was stranded on the sandbank for four continuous weeks. The loneliness finally told on his nerves. In desperation, he left the barge and lived in the forest on the bank, in a camouflaged house, composed of tarpaulins. This was chiefly due to his barge having been bombed in error by one of our own aeroplanes. A few days later his Russian escort to the Bolo prisoners deserted. He then retired to the barge, which he placed in what he termed a state of defence, with three Vickers' guns he had discovered in the forest. He had no knowledge of how to fire them, but as he had no belts and no small-arms ammunition for them, even that knowledge would have been of little use.

The evolutions of the motor boat owned by the D.A.D.S. and T. was another amazing sight on the river. The two peasants in charge were completely ignorant of motors. Furthermore, they knew nothing of the river, and when operating the boat watched neither the sandbanks nor the crafts they were ordered to make for. They usually ended up quite 300 yards past the barge they were bound for. Upon touching a sandbank, the sole remedy of the so-called engineers was to go ahead, hoping thereby to get over. The usual result was that the vessel went high and dry.

The D.A.D.S. and T. lost his temper ; the Russians grew sullen, and the final result was that the D.A.D.S. and T., his batman, his interpreter, and the Russian engineers, all stripped naked, would persuade the grounded craft to float again.

One morning the launch performed extraordinary feats. Attempts were made to go ahead. Nothing happened, except that the vessel drifted down-stream with the current. Upon an inquiry being made, the engineer quietly pointed out that he had dropped his two propellers in midstream some time during the previous evening !

CHAPTER II

HOW THE NAVY HELPED US.

" LIAISON " is a French word. But the process of carrying out the duties appertaining to the word is fraught with interest and delight. Liaison between the Navy and the Army on the Dvina was amazingly close. It is seldom that the Silent Service speaks. But a Naval description of the above-mentioned process should go down to posterity.

Being in ignorance of the exact meaning of the term, the Navy, upon being ordered to go ashore and perform liaison duties with the Army, saluted, turned about, and proceeded ashore.

Thus they continued in their recital :—

" On our way to the quarters we were to occupy we encountered various army officers in stages of undress. These appeared to be friendly. So far, good. Our quarters consisted of a loft with very indifferent flooring. If we trod on the plank nearest to the front door, we upset the lime-juice in the opposite corner of the room. Similarly, each plank trodden upon upset something at a distance. Some planks were higher than others. This meant that they sank more. But they all upset something. The roof existed in places.

" The quarters had a great many good points, however, which far outweighed the bad ones. To start with, if you spilt anything, there was no need to worry about it making a mess of the drawing-room carpet. It was certain to drop on the sheep which lived in the stables underneath. If we wanted to regard the weather, there was no need to go out into the street. A clear view of three-fourths of the sky could be obtained from the armchair by merely tilting the head back slightly. At night one always knew at once if it started to rain. And in the morning our valet had only to walk twice across the drawing-room to sweep its floor as clean as a whistle. Again, when we were awakened at 3 a.m. by a cat, there was nothing to prevent opening fire on it with a ·450.

" There were great points in those quarters. We spent several very good days' duck shooting. Then we were rung up and asked why the —— we weren't doing liaison, and why we had sent in no information to the ship. Also, why the —— ! ! !

" We placed our receiver back on its hook, hung our revolver on the telephone bell, and sat down to think.

" We came to the conclusion that liaison must mean —(1) To dress as a naval officer ; (2) to challenge everyone who passed. We could think of no other points in which we had failed in our duty. The Army's idea of the Navy is universally acknowledged as being that they are a strange race of creatures who wear baggy trousers, which they hitch up at frequent intervals, exclaim ' Yo ! ho !' at more frequent intervals, drink rum, and swear horribly. We had a pair of baggy trousers ; we got a belt which necessitated hitching them up ; and we put in an urgent request for rum.

In view of having all these points in our favour, we considered that we might dispense with the ' Yo ! ho's !'

" The question of information was easily disposed of by ringing up the Intelligence Officer and inviting him to dinner. His arrival coincided with that of the rum. We obtained a mass of quite unreliable information from him, and sent it on to the ship, who were not in a position to judge of its worth. The sentries were meanwhile busily challenging all passing officers, who advanced with one accord to be recognized. Having been recognized and introduced, they remained. The departure of all Army officers synchronized exactly with that of the last of the rum.

" We inquired of several of them what the meaning of ' liaison ' was. The most coherent answer was to the effect that it was ' Getting matey with the Army, old bean.' We therefore asked other officers to dine, and on one occasion two of them set off together for their quarters some fifty yards away. They were found next morning sleeping peacefully in the middle of a potato patch in H.Q. village (distant roughly five miles). On our return to the ship shortly afterwards we were informed that the liaison was very good."

But the Silent Service did more than liaison work on land : they managed the 60-pounder guns. The history of the 60-pounders, the one baptized and the other just a heathen, must be fully told. It opens with the embarkation of the 5-ton 60-pounder on H.M.S. *Oil Drum II*. The Royal Engineers, with many

Russian soldier assistants, succeeded after much cursing and " *neyte dobras* " to load the gun. The *Levic* then towed the *Oil Drum* as far as Gunners' Bridge, where the Services proposed to land the 60-pounder.

In Russia, however much the Services propose, native tugs and the skippers thereof invariably dispose. The *Levic*, with true Russian nonchalance, became too exhausted to tow the *Oil Drum* close into the shore. Lengthy consultations ensued. It was decided to pull the *Oil Drum* inshore by ropes, which were duly affixed—work at which Lieut. Davis, of beach fame, proved remarkably assiduous. Then the strain began.

This sudden spasm of effort aroused the torpid *Levic*. She made an expiring effort, which, instead of producing a favourable result, merely caused poor Davis's ropes to become fouled in some of the numerous angles of the *Oil Drum*. With quiet and dignified grace the vessel turned over, and the 60-pounder slid into sixteen feet of Dvina water, where it disintegrated into its various component parts.

The gun, however, was not abandoned, but by means of divers and cranes, and the skill of the Royal Navy, was fished up and put together again. As a reward for their good work, the Navy were permitted to drag the gun from Luby's Landing some thousand yards, use it, and drag it back again.

To use the gun the seamen had to observe their shooting. This they did naturally from a church, as we were at war. In far-away peaceful France one never used a church as an observation post! (Well, hardly ever!)

With much doubt as to the strength of the R.E. ladders, and more vituperation as to the way they were rigged, the observers eventually reached a glorified dovecot at the top of the church steeple, complete with two holes for entry and exit of doves or purposes of observation. Various telephones, most of them apparently out of order, and a heated corporal endeavouring to buzz up, completed the party.

If one moved a foot to the right, one fell down the ladder. A foot to the left the floor was apparently solid, but in reality was a most ingenious trapdoor of the best baronial type of six hundred years ago. The corporal explained that the R.E. had run out of nails, and had gone to Archangel to get a packet, the Ordnance Department having none.

"Well, there you are, old thing! In front of the village and over to the left you see a yellow sandbank. There's a trench all along the top of it, and that cutting in the middle is a road coming down it. On the left of the cutting there's a black slit. That's a M.G. post. Now go right, about 300 yards. You see a clump of trees and a bank with a cemetery on top just to the right of it. There's a M.G. in a blockhouse on the edge of the bank close to the trees, and a trench running round the back of the trees to the village, and various blockhouses and trenches along the cemetery to the right." The speaker was the military liaison officer.

"Right you are. We'll have a lap at the M.G. post

on the left of the cutting at 15.00 hours. It's easy to see, and clear all round, and my observing officer doesn't know this place yet, so we may as well register there as anywhere."

Three o'clock sees the party once more in the dove-cot. The landscape is just the same, with the addition of a herd of cows and an old man wandering down in front of the cutting. Frantic buzzing on the telephone.

" Is the 60-pounder ready yet ?"

" Another five minutes."

" Tell the C.O. that he should hurry up as much as possible."

The cows wander down to the water, drink, and very slowly return, the old man leading the way. At this moment the gun reports ready.

" All right. Got your range and deflection ? Right-o ! Fire !"

The tower rocks slightly, and a colossal cloud of black smoke arrives about 100 yards behind the last cow. Inside three seconds the old man is a bad last, and the cows are half-way to the woods, with their tails pointing to the skies. Much chuckling among the doves.

" Up 400. Fire !"

Another cloud, behind the cutting this time.

" Down 200. Fire !"

Right at the foot of the cutting.

" That's splendid. Right at the bottom of the bank and within twenty yards of the post. Give her five rounds rapid."

The first drops at the bottom of the blockhouse, and each succeeding one goes about 200 yards farther over than the last. The fifth round drops about twenty-five yards in front of a house in the village. The smoke clears away; an old woman comes out of the house, takes in her washing, and goes in again.

It is explained in vehement tones to the gunlayers to keep to the same target, and not put the sights up after each shot. The gunners explain back in most indignant tones that their sights are perfectly set, and are not moved without orders. Furthermore, that the gun jumps badly. Back-chat ensues on the subject of hanging rum breakers on it to keep it down. " Were they going to Bisley next year ? What did we know about 60-pounders, anyway ?"—a most unfortunate sally, as they knew quite as little.

Eventually one more round at the same target, same range and deflection.

" Fire !"

A beautiful cloud rises up some 300 yards to the right of the target, and right on top of the M.G. position in the cemetery.

" Rapid fire !"

" How many rounds ?"

" All you've got."

And away go some eight rounds, each about 100 yards longer than the last, with pleasing glimpses of Bolos running like redshanks between the bursts. Ammunition runs out, and everyone goes home to laugh.

Extract from next day's communique :—

"Our naval 60-pounders bombarded cemetery position yesterday with great accuracy, causing Bolo to run from his trenches."

But the sailormen did not always have 60-pounders to blaze off at the Bolo. Later in the campaign they descended to 12-pounders, admittedly naval ones. Even with those they made matters warm for the enemy.

On the river the Navy had its own trouble. Mines were a terrible trial. The whole river was sown with them, and during the early days after the outbreak of the mutiny in Dyer's Battalion the *Sword Dance* and the *Fandango* were blown up. One man was killed in the former, and one officer and seven other ratings in the latter.

The enemy endeavoured to float mines down the river on to the flotilla off Troitsa, and a net defence was therefore constructed and laid across the river up stream.

In securing one of these mines which was floating down towards a hospital barge, Lieut. R. H. Fitz-herbert-Brockholes, R.N., and three ratings were blown up.

Perhaps it is as well, as this is a record, to detail the happenings in connection with the flotilla on the Dvina.

The four gunboats (H.M.S's. *Cockchafer*, *Cicala*, *Cricket*, and *Glow-worm*) and H.M.'s Monitors "M. 23" and "M. 25" had wintered at Archangel and, after being reconditioned, proceeded up river as soon as the heavy ice had run early in May, and from then onwards the flotilla continued in support of the Army until the river was blocked by our mines immediately before evacuation.

The flotilla, then under command of the late Commander Sebald W. B. Green, D.S.O., R.N., assisted in the retaking of Tulgas on May 18th.

On June 3rd Captain Edward Altham, C.B., R.N., who had come out ahead of the naval reinforcements, arrived up river and took command of the flotilla.

At this time hopes were entertained of assisting the Russians to reach Kotlas and join hands with Koltchak. In view of this and the necessity for keeping the shallow-draught gunboats in reserve, it was necessary to employ the deeper-draught monitors as much as possible.

H.M.S. *Humber* and H.M. Monitors " M. 27," " M. 31," and " M. 33," arrived from England early in June and joined the advanced flotilla. The gunboats were sent in pairs to refit at Archangel.

On June 19th a more extensive operation was undertaken, with the object of capturing the high ground between Topsa and Troitsa, and the flotilla co-operated with Graham's Brigade, bombarding heavily prior to the attack, and countering the fire of the enemy ships, of which a number were armed with heavy long-range guns.

H.M.S. *Cockchafer* (Lieut.-Commander Quintin B. Preston-Thomas, R.N.) did particularly good work in getting up the narrow Kurgomin channel within a mile of Topsa when that place was taken, and materially assisted in repulsing a counter-attack which threatened the success of our undertakings.

H.M.S. *Glow-worm* (Commander S. W. B. Green, D.S.O., R.N.) was actively engaged with the enemy ships in the main river.

H.M.S. *Humber*, H.M's. " M.27 " and " M.33 " also assisted in this operation which marked the first definite stage of the advance, and materially improved our tactical positions.

This brought the ships to the edge of the enemy minefield, and for the next week minesweeping had to be carried out under most difficult conditions. The river water was so thick, it was impossible to see any appreciable depth, even from a seaplane.

Instead of being able to sweep in comparative safety on the rise of tide as at sea, the river was, of course, tideless and falling. It was necessary to explore channels with small steamboats, clear mines where discovered, buoy them, and then send up the heavier-draught tunnel minesweepers to sweep up the heavier and deeper moored mines.

The whole of the work had to be done within range of the enemy flotilla, and the minesweeping craft were daily under heavy fire from his guns, and at times even came under direct machine-gun and rifle fire.

By June 27th a passage had been swept to Troitsa, and H.M.S. *Cricket* (Lieut. Ion W. G. White, R.N.), with Brigadier-General F. W. H. Walshe, Brigadier-General General Staff, and the Senior Naval Officer River, on board, ran through a heavy barrage from the enemy guns and arrived off that place, where the high cliffs provided some measure of protection.

The following day, the enemy ships having been driven back by our gunboats' fire, the remainder of the flotilla and transport moved up to Troitsa, which from then onwards was our advanced base and Brigade Headquarters.

On July 7th, when the mutiny broke out in Dyer's Battalion, and the 4th North Russian Rifles became affected, fifty seamen, under Commander Frank G. Bramble, R.N., and a small Royal Marine detachment, under Lieut. Clive M. Sergeant, R.M., were landed at the General Officer Commanding's request, to assist in securing our position until the arrival of more British troops.

The enemy, who was evidently fully conversant with the situation, seized the opportunity to attack.

The night of July 7th–8th the situation was critical, as British reinforcements had not arrived. The Russian troops were disaffected, or in no heart to fight, and the enemy's gunboats were pressing hard in support of his shore advance on the right bank.

Very valuable assistance had been rendered by the seaplanes, bombing and machine-gunning, but by the forenoon of July 8th they had " run out," and had to be given a brief rest and overhaul.

The situation about this time was that the enemy were reported within 1,200 yards of the flotilla anchorage and seaplane base, with the Russians slowly retiring.

The auxiliary craft and seaplanes were therefore

moved back, and H.M.S. *Humber*, which had been covering Topsa during the mutiny, came up-river and embarked the Senior Naval Officer.

A telephone cable was run to the shore to keep n close touch with the General Officer Commanding (Brigadier-General L. W. de V. Sadleir-Jackson, C.B., C.M.G., D.S.O.), who had by now taken over the command.

H.M. " M. 33 " was hit by a heavy shell, fortunately without casualties, and continued in action. H.M. " M. 27 " did useful service with her triple 4-inch mounting.

H.M.S. *Cicala* (Lieut. E. T. Grayston, R.N.R.), who had been heavily engaged as advanced gunboat, developed defects due to the continual firing at high elevation, and was relieved by H.M.S. *Cricket*.

The latter ship came under heavy machine-gun fire from the woods in the vicinity of Selmenga, but replied to it with her own machine guns, and moved farther up-river—the channel leading away from the wooded bank—and continued to engage the enemy ships.

That afternoon H.M.S. *Cricket* was hit on the water-line with a heavy shell, and had to come down-river and secure alongside the repair barges, as there appeared to be a risk of the ship sinking.

The gap had to be filled promptly to prevent the enemy profiting by his success. H.M.S. *Humber* (Lieut.-Commander Andrew Johnstone, R.N.) slipped cable and telephone and proceeded up-river full speed until stopped by her deeper draught. The fire of her

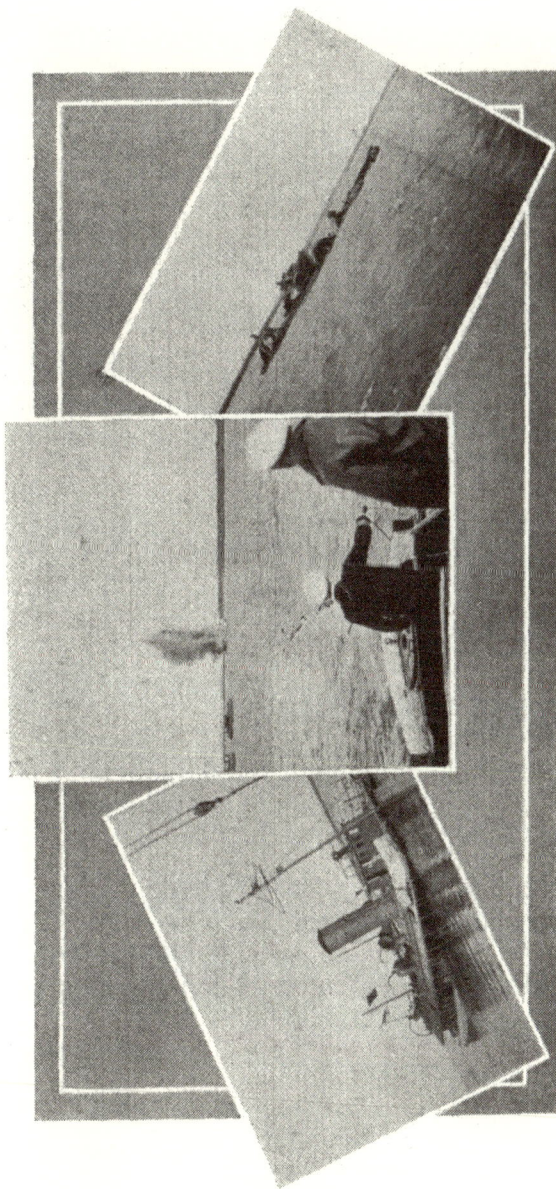

THE SUNKEN SHIP.   THE MINE EXPLOSION.   THE RESULT.

H.M.S. "Sword Dance" (Lieut. A. K. McC. Halliley, D.S.O., R.N.) before, during and after the Explosion of the Destructiv
Charges on Sept. 10th, when it was found impossible to salve her completely in time for the Final Evacuation.
Captain Altham, C.B., Senior Naval Officer River) can be seen watching the Explosion of the Charge.

twin 6-inch turret was so effective that, with the further assistance of seaplanes' bombing, the enemy flotilla's fire was silenced, and it withdrew.

That evening a counter-attack was organized to be carried out by the Russian troops, and four heavy bombardments were carried out by the monitors, but very little progress was made, the Russians showing little inclination to fight.

As there were still no signs of the British troops, the naval paddle-steamers and *Borodino* (Senior Naval Officer's ship) were dispatched to assist in bringing them up, and on the morning of July 9th they arrived, and the position was stabilized.

In the course of the minesweeping operations involved in the advance, H.M. tunnel minesweepers *Sword Dance* (Lieut. Alan K. McC. Halliley, R.N.) and *Fandango* (Chief Boatswain Thomas J. Vosper, R.N.) were mined and sunk, with the loss of one rating killed in the former, and one officer and seven ratings in the latter.

Over forty mines were swept up or recovered.

None can tell the story of the trials and tribulations of the Naval Service better than themselves, and it is left to one of the flotilla officers to describe some of their experiences.

" We were unfortunate," he says, " in missing the capture of Topsa, having been sent down to Archangel to have the mountings of our two Mark VII 6-inch guns altered so as to give them an increase of range, without which we were unable to compete with the Bolo gunboats, which up to that time outranged us

E

by about 1,500 yards. Indeed, they had actually
shelled us out of our anchorage at Gunner's Bridge
without our being able to make an effective reply.

" By chipping away a part of the mounting, the
elevation of the gun could be increased, and an addition of 2,600 yards given to the range, which gave a
maximum range of 16,100 yards.

" We arrived back at Gunner's Bridge on June 23rd.
It had formerly been a somewhat unsafe spot, when the
Bolo overlooked it from the cliffs of Troitsa, but now
it seemed a pleasant rural retreat, as calm and peaceful
as the Thames at Marlowe.

" However, the very first night—if one can speak
of ' night ' at that time of the year, when three hours
of twilight separate sunset from sunrise—our dreams
of peace and quiet were rudely dispelled by a Bolo
plane which dropped a couple of bombs between us
and the bank, the closer one giving the ship a nasty
jolt, and spattering the forecastle with splinters.

" A few days later we relieved H.M.S. *Cicala* in the
advanced position, about five miles farther up. There
our job was to support H.M. Mine-sweepers *Step-Dance*
and *Fandango*, which were operating at the bend of
the river below the high red bluff of Troitsa. H.M.S.
Sword Dance had been blown up by a mine a few
days before, and the wreck lay a couple of cables astern
of us, with her upper works and square stern sticking
out of the water.

"On the starboard side was a small flat island, covered
with scrub, and behind that a broad meadow, with
pine forests at the back.   These pine forests effectually

screened us from the enemy. From a little distance
the green-painted gunboat was hardly to be distinguished against the background.

" Had it not been for the restless activity of the
' Dancing Class,' as the Quartermaster always announced them, we should have enjoyed perfect peace ;
but as soon as they got under weigh the trouble always
started. Whenever the Quartermaster announced,
' The " Dancing Class " weighing, sir,' everyone swore
softly or sighed resignedly, according to temperament.

" The Bolos had that corner spotted to a nicety,
probably from the tall green spire of the church at
Yakolevskoe, a little village about seven miles farther
up on the left bank.

" Whenever H.M.Ms. *Step-Dance* and *Fandango*, pre-
ceded by the two little ' searching ' steamboats, showed
themselves beyond the bend of the river, it was only
a matter of seconds before a lofty column of spray and
a distant boom told that the Bolo was busy. But
nothing could discourage those sweepers. Time after
time the sweep would part, and they would manœuvre,
slowly and deliberately, in the narrow mine-infested
channel, without the slightest regard for the shells
falling all round them, join up a new sweep, and carry
on. One square hit from a 5.9 would have meant
practical annihilation, and they frequently escaped only
by a matter of a very few yards.

" The gunboat would then advance close under the
bank to a position just short of the point and open
fire, with the object of diverting the enemy's attention,
usually with a success which, I have no doubt, should

have been a source of great satisfaction to us. He seemed to think we were in the meadow before mentioned, and used to ' savage ' it thoroughly, and then thoughtfully search the river. Our shooting from this position was, of course, all indirect fire, the spotting being done by the observation post on Troitsa Bluff or by a seaplane.

" As the sweepers cleared the channel farther up, it was necessary for us to follow close astern of them and come out into the open at the bend of the river, where one looked up a long, straight vista—high red cliffs on the left, and low meadowland and sandbanks on the right, and terminated in the hazy distance by a low-lying neck of land, over which you could see the smoke of the Bolo gunboats as they moved to and fro.

" Under these circumstances, the chief distraction of those not actually employed in fighting the ship was to stand by with a landing-net to scoop in the dead fish which drifted past, killed by the shell bursts ahead. There were a great number of them, chiefly pike and bream, and both were excellent eating—a blessed relief from the eternal bully beef and tinned salmon. The excitement was sometimes intense as a good specimen came drifting down—men rushing from one side to the other, uncertain which side of the stern it was going to pass. Sometimes it would drift past just out of reach of the long pole ; or else, just as it was about to be netted, it would suddenly wake up, give a flip with its tail, and dive gleefully into the depths. One really Heath-Robinson incident occurred. A stoker, assisted—or, rather, hindered—by an excited crowd of his pals, all shouting advice at the same time, was craning out over the rail, trying to land a particularly fine pike with a little net (made from a 'sweat-rag') on the end of a pole about 10 feet long, when suddenly—'Whiz! Plonk! Bang!'—a 4-inch shell landed as nearly as possible in his net; in fact, between the net and the ship's side. Anyhow, it scorched the paint and scored the side with splinters. Expecting to find a horrible scene of carnage, I jumped down on to the main deck. There wasn't a soul to be seen—only the pale face of the late fisherman peering doubtfully round the corner of the engine-room casing. Though they all got a pretty drenching, not one was touched, and five minutes afterwards they were all fishing as enthusiastically as ever.

" On June 27th, as the Senior Naval Officer of the river had promised to secure for the General a much-desired landing-place for troops in Troitsa Bay, which was under direct observation of the enemy gunboats, and well within their range, H.M.S. *Cricket* was told off to advance and drive them back out of range. H.M.S. *Cricket* and H.M.S. *Cicala* were the only two ships at that time which had the necessary range, and, unfortunately, H.M.S. *Cicala's* foremost gun was out of action. We had therefore only one 6-inch gun to oppose four or five Bolo gun-boats, not to mention land batteries at Selmenga and Seltso on their respective sides of the river.

" We opened fire at 10 a.m. in support of the minesweepers which were clearing the last of that particular mine-field. The day was a perfect one for a river picnic—dead calm and blazing hot, with a clear blue sky and a few fleecy clouds reflected in the glassy surface of the river. With the bright red cliffs on the left and the cool green meadow and pine woods on the right, it made a very pretty picture.

" As the Bolo shells came whistling overhead or exploded with an ear-splitting crack on the water ahead, astern, and on either side, and the splinters came dropping out of the blue—' p-fit, p-fit '—knocking up little white spurts of spray, the crashing report of our own 6-inch gun shook the ship like a jelly, and the hot, acrid cordite smoke dried one's mouth and throat, and the blazing sun beat down on the iron decks. How one longed to get into those cool green woods, and burrow into the bushes away from it all !

" Hour after hour it went on, steadily and with deliberation. As the Bolo found our range, we shifted slowly from place to place, keeping carefully in the swept channel, and giving a wide berth to the left bank, where the ugly spiked heads of a number of large sea mines were just visible on the surface.

" About 4 p.m. the time came to make a dash round the corner into Troitsa Bay. We switched on full speed and forged ahead against the strong current, using every ounce of steam to get as quickly as possible through the spot where the enemy was putting down a barrage on the narrow channel between the bank and the mines. As the ship gathered speed, making rapid fire with the forward 6-inch gun, a shell crashed down on our quarter, missing the stern by a few yards ; it must have barely cleared the mast-head in its descent. Next a great pillar of spray shot up ahead, directly in our track, followed in a few seconds by another in the same spot, now a few yards short of our bow, and as we steamed through the black swirl a shower of spray and splinters descended on the decks and all around.

" What an eternity we seemed dragging our length through that spot !

" By all the rules of the game, the next should have landed fair and square on the quarter-deck, but he didn't get it off in time—he probably had a missfire—and the few extra seconds allowed us to get clear, as the next one, faultless for direction, burst well astern. Swerving to port, we ran into the little bay, where we were either invisible to the enemy or else well camouflaged against the background. He still continued to put them down in the same place, and searched the lower side of the bay, evidently using the ruined belfry of Topsa Church as his aiming mark. But they all passed harmlessly over us. Here we anchored—and a soldier swam out to have a ' look-see !'

" The object was not yet accomplished, however, as the enemy was still within easy range of the spot where it was desired to establish the landing-stage.

" H.M. Monitor ' M. 83 ' now came up, and we replenished ammunition from her, and again advanced, reaching by about 8 p.m. a position about three miles farther up, which remained the ' advanced position ' until the capture of Seltso, a couple of months afterwards.

" By that time the enemy had become discouraged,

and we ceased fire at 8.30 p.m., and Troitsa Bay remained the Naval and Military Advanced Base until the evacuation.

" On the night of the mutiny of Dyer's Battalion— July 7th—after a prolonged stay in the advanced position, during which we had frequent petty tiffs with the Bolo, we returned to Troitsa Bay at 6 p.m. for a ' stand-easy.'

" At 3 a.m. orders were received for the landing-party, comprising every man who could be spared, to stand by ; but it did not land, as at 4 a.m. we were ordered to open rapid fire on the woods on the right bank with 3-inch shells at 4,000 yards. It was just getting daylight, and a hasty evacuation was taking place of the hospital on the edge of the wood, from which came the steady clatter of machine-gun fire of the advancing Bolos. Russian soldiers could be seen retreating in quick time out of the wood—while a section of twenty sailors, with machine guns over their shoulders, were marching in ; wounded were being carried down on stretchers to a barge alongside the bank, and the seaplanes drawn up on the beach were being hastily cranked up. It was a scene of great animation, viewed from the comparative safety of the gunboat.

" The enemy gunboats, however, soon began to take a hand in the business, and we therefore advanced, in company with H.M. ' M. 33,' to engage them, and a pretty hot action followed. We took up a position close under the cliffs of the right bank, where continuous machine-gun fire still resounded through the woods, but at a good distance inland. The enemy seemed to have got our position well marked off, and was getting unpleasantly close. We therefore shifted our position and closed the range. Just as we passed under the stern of H.M. 'M. 33,' a cloud of black smoke shot up from her amidships, and it was evident she was hit. She was not badly damaged, the shot having only destroyed the ward-room, sparing the wine store, as the captain cheerfully informed us as we passed. Together we continued the action for another half-hour or so, shifting from place to place, and the enemy, according to his usual tactics, ceased fire and retired behind his river bank. However, he was soon out again, and several more small strafes occurred ; but about 10 a.m. he packed up, and we were able to get some breakfast. Between 11 a.m. and 12 noon we were again ordered to fire on positions on the right bank, where his artillery was annoying the troops, and by 12.15 p.m. all was quiet, and we anchored in the usual advanced position.

" As we had received reports that the enemy had retired to his original position, on the far bank of the Selmenga stream, we looked forward to a quiet afternoon, and possibly a little sleep ; in fact, most of the men were below, ' getting their heads down,' when at 1 p.m., without the slightest warning, a perfect storm of machine-gun and rifle fire broke out from the woods on the bank, at a range of about 50 yards. The few on deck scuttled for cover, or froze like rabbits behind anything handy.

" For what seemed a very long time, but was probably only a few minutes, the enemy had it all his own way, the bullets beating on the side and upper works with a deafening clatter, like the noise of an automatic riveter, sweeping across the deck and lashing the water into foam on the lee side. We were at anchor, and it was perfectly obvious that no one could have reached the forecastle alive to slip the anchor, nor could as much as one round have been got off from the guns, as the crews are entirely exposed, and must have been wiped out in a few seconds; and the machine guns on the engaged side were equally unprotected. However, a couple of Lewis guns were got across from the disengaged side and poked round corners, and were soon adding to the general din.

"In a few minutes H.M. 'M. 27,' anchored some distance astern of us, opened fire with salvos of triple 3-inch. This diversion enabled us to slip our anchor and shift to the other side of the river, where we again anchored. During the next few days about 250 dead Bolos were found in the wood.

"In the ship there were only two men wounded, which was extraordinary good luck, as the upper works, bridge, and funnels were riddled with bullet-holes—I counted 150 and then gave it up—and several had gone straight through the plating of the ship's side.

"During the afternoon continuous sniping went on from the bank. You had only to put your head above the hatch or show yourself for a moment on deck, and a bullet would come across. There was one persistent gent—evidently an officer of Dyer's Battalion, as he was wearing khaki and a Sam Browne belt —who seemed determined to do some one in. He could be seen constantly dodging from cover to cover.

Our gunner had a long argument with him with a Lewis gun, but the duel ended without a score.

" At 4 p.m. the enemy gunboats opened fire again, and the same weary business went on. By 4.15 p.m. they had got our range, and began to get unpleasant, and we therefore weighed and advanced up the river towards Seltso as far as we dared, on account of the mines, which had not been swept any further. In this position we were receiving the fire of the batteries at Selmenga on the right bank, from a battery of 3-inch guns at Seltso on the left bank, and from the Bolo gunboats ahead, as well as numerous small stuff that came buzzing about in an impertinent way from Lord knows where. Speaking for himself, the writer began to get the ' scatters,' because the beastly things came from all directions, and there was no ' lee ' anywhere.

" I have heard men say that they have never ' ducked.' Well, to my mind, there are two occasions on which one ' ducks.' Firstly, when the projectile goes so close that you just hear the whizz and bang ; it is impossible to say which comes first. This is merely a reflex action—involuntary, and not to be attributed to funk. The second is when the splinters fly and you ' duck ' behind any cover that may be handy, which is only common sense. The man who has never ' ducked ' has never had a shell close enough to him.

" It became quite obvious that we could not continue to dodge them for long, and at 4.40 p.m. a 5.9-inch shell hit us amidships on the starboard side under the water line. The shock was hardly greater than that given by a shell bursting in the water close to the ship, but the deluge of water on deck and the oil-fuel gushing from the ship's side left no room for doubt.

" The ship then took a sharp list to starboard, and was evidently sinking, so the only thing to do was to retire and endeavour to beach her out of range. We therefore started to turn in the narrow channel, and got the after gun into action. Unfortunately, the additional draught given by the list and the amount of water in the ship caused us to ground on a sand-bank—directly under the cliffs where we had been so badly shot up earlier in the day and the woods were still ringing with machine-gun fire. As we stuck on the bank, broadside on to the enemy, he fired faster than ever, correcting his range to within yards. The next ten minutes were excessively unpleasant.

" It was with enormous relief that we saw the bow gradually paying off and the ship moving again.

" Once afloat, we legged it down river, firing our after gun, and the enemy shots following—ahead, astern, and on both sides—the water creeping up and up, in spite of the pumps, till the engines were heaving round in three feet of water. In ten minutes or so we reached Troitsa Bay, a few hundred yards beyond the enemy's extreme range, a few minutes before the fires were put out and everything stopped. And such was the end of a perfect day !"

In connection with the work of the naval forces one might mention the work of the Mercantile Marine, who played their part—and at times an unpleasant part—in the campaign.

The *Walton Belle* before the fateful year of 1914 was a paddle-steamer at Margate. Eventually she arrived in the Dvina, and in an emergency was used to convey supposedly loyal Russian troops to deal with a difficult situation at Onega. The vessel was manned by unarmed mercantile marine ratings. The Russian troops were thoroughly equipped, and armed with rifles and Lewis guns.

On arriving at Onega, at that time in the hands of the Bolshevik mutineers, the First Lieutenant, with two men, went ashore, and with a Lewis gun cleared the village in the vicinity of the docks. The loyal Russians, armed to the teeth, could not be induced to follow. Delaying pins and other persuasive weapons finally resulted in a few going ashore. The First Lieutenant, being then in possession of several Bolshevik prisoners, finding the Russians unwilling to follow, abandoned his attack. He realized, and very wisely, that it was hardly possible to capture the town with two other ratings.

The Bolsheviks, having now recovered from their first alarms, counter-attacked, and the *Walton Belle* escaped from Onega under heavy shell and machine-gun fire.

On the voyage back to Archangel the four or five Bolo prisoners succeeded in disarming their guard, threw a bomb at the Captain, and proceeded to clean up the ship. They completely subdued the 200 heavily armed Russians. The situation was entirely in favour of the Bolsheviks till it was taken in hand by one of the mercantile marine ratings, who appeared on deck with a shot-gun and blew the heads off two of the mutineers, one with the right barrel and the other with the left.

This subdued the state of turmoil till the port was reached. Considerable excitement was created by her arrival. S O S signals were being fired, and Lewis guns and rifles were being discharged on the unfortunate paddle-steamer.

A boarding party from H.M.S. *Fox* finally subdued the excited and mutinous Russians, and it is not to be wondered at that the men from the *Fox* did not discriminate in the meting out of punishment to both the Bolshevik and the so-called loyal Russian.

Naval transport officers were always being fixed up with things. The story is told of a certain R.A.F. officer who superintended the loading of a barge. The river was at this time extraordinarily low. A N.T.O. arrived to find the deck of the barge piled high with cases of every description.

" Why the hell have you put all this stuff on deck ?" inquired the N.T.O. " Is it all full down below ?"

R.A.F. Officer : " No. I haven't put anything down below."

N.T.O. : " Why not ?"

R.A.F. Officer : " Well, you see, they told me there wasn't much water in the river, so I put all the stuff on deck to keep the barge from being loaded too deep and drawing too much water !"

Collapse of N.T.O.

The following was received almost daily from the First Lieutenant, *Borodino* :—

" How many *barishynas* can you let me have to-morrow, old boy ?"

N.T.O., to Beach Officer : " Fix the First Lieutenant, *Borodino*, up with a few women to-morrow, will you ?"

SCENE : N.T.O.'s office. Confusion worse confused. Telephones ringing. Interpreters arguing with carpenters. N.T.Os. harangueing *barishynas*. Beach Officer cursing Russians.

N.T.O., arriving : " Hello !   What's all this about ?"

Chorus : " Davis has lost his horse."

The *barishynas* had been employed during one afternoon loading a Carbus with small-arms ammunition. The loading was completed at 6 p.m.

At eight the next morning the N.T.O, was informed that the Carbus was full of water. A tug was sent alongside to pump it out. At ten o'clock the N.T.O. himself went down to the beach, and found the Carbus still full of water, and the tug still pumping hard.

He ordered the tug to beach the Carbus. This was done, the Carbus coming right up on the beach, and it was discovered that the bottom of the barge had dropped out in the night, and the tug had been attempting to pump out the Dvina !

Over the telephone :—N.T.O. : " Can you send the quickest and most comfortable launch you have to Seltso to pick up Prince Morousi ?"

N.T.O. to interpreter : " Send the *Coffin* to Seltso for Prince Morousi, will you ?"

The difficulty of the fresh meat-supply was more

easily solved by our naval friends than by ourselves. Our consciences were not so elastic. Cattle and sheep strolled about in a most tantalizing manner in all parts of the line, save " No Man's Land." Animal sagacity may have been responsible for their avoidance of that area, yet they gathered in large numbers on the river banks. The natural result was a distinct difference in naval and military diets.

Only once in the campaign did we secure a cow. One with suicidal tendencies, weary of the dull monotony of Russian life, succeeded in strangling itself in an intricate mass of barbed wire. Whatever the motives actuating the animal happened to be, its self-sacrifice was most deeply appreciated by all neighbouring messes. The event, however, brought forth copious tears from the unfortunate peasant owner (a war widow). Compensation eventually matured in the shape of a new cow, a gift which resulted in the kissing of the feet of any British officer who ventured in or near the gratified woman's dwelling. But it was not always as easy to deal with the Russian peasant. Selling surplus horses fell to the lot of the D.A.D.S. and T., Major Watson. To call the populace together, one warns all the *storastas* (headmen). The time and place of the sale are notified. Large numbers of bewhiskered Russian peasants gather at the appointed time. The first horse is displayed. The peasant desiring to purchase asks what price the seller is willing to accept. The latter names a price double that which he expects eventually to receive.

The peasant walks away and ponders on the matter.

OUR PRISONERS.

A few of the Bolsheviks we captured on August 10th in the Cage on Troitsa Beach.

After some meditation he returns and offers about half
what he is prepared to give.

" No, no," the seller answers.

A long explanation is at once commenced by the
prospective buyer, in which he points out the unfortunate weather that has been experienced, the failure of
the crop, the abnormal size of his family—anything
that will conduce to the consideration of a reduction
in price. The actual price asked is never queried. But
the explanations of misfortune multiply.

The buyer retorts that the offer is absurd, and walks
away. Eventually the peasant returns and makes a
fresh offer, which is again rejected. This performance
continues, being repeated and repeated, sometimes
prolonged for several hours, till the Russian makes a
fair offer for the animal, which is promptly accepted.
Time is nothing to the Russian ; to-morrow is as good
as to-day. It is evident that a particular buyer means
to secure a particular horse, and the only method of
sale is to be untiringly obstinate, till he eventually offers
a reasonable figure. And the Russian is an expert at
judging horses and their value.

The Russian peasantry is extraordinarily superstitious. The one curious example that came directly
under my notice was in connection with the pigeon,
though at the actual time I was ignorant of its signifi-
cance.

We had been shooting duck on the left bank of the
river in the early morning. Returning to Mutiny Village, a number of pigeons were seen, feeding in the
track ahead. The possibility of ownership deterred us

F

from disturbing and shooting them. Inquiries among the villagers produced the welcome news that the birds were no one's property and were wild. Proposals to shoot them, however, met with a copious flow of tears from one peasant woman, who pitifully entreated us to allow the birds to live. All attempts to discover a reason for this sudden outburst merely resulted in more tears and cries of anguish. A few mornings after the same peasant woman was observed feeding the so-called wild pigeons with dried peas. The incident passed from our minds.

Months afterwards I learned the explanation. The Russian peasantry, though outwardly most devout and religious, retain nevertheless several remarkable superstitious beliefs. One of the most prevalent is that on death the soul of the departed passes into, and for three weeks remains in, the body of a pigeon. The bereaved relatives and friends, ignorant of the identity of the possessed pigeon, feed for the allotted time all pigeons in the village, in the earnest hope that they may give sustenance to the particular pigeon containing the soul of the departed.

The death of that pigeon means the complete death of the soul—why, I have never been able to discover. The peasant woman of many tears and signs had had the misfortune, in the attack on Troitsa, to lose her son and her infant babe through shell fire. Hence the tears and protestations, a singular example of the persistence of an ancient superstition.

There was one famous house, Dobra-Ville. Some of the Navy made it their permanent residence, and

they shall tell the story of the wondrous house-
hold :—

" The owners of Dobra-Ville were rather naturally
the Dobras, whose real name was Gregorian-Jugoff,
and their offspring was legion. These good folk occupied one room, and some of them slept in the barn
behind, which was also shared by a horse, a prehistoric
rowing boat, and a multitude of small insects.

" When we first arrived they rather kept to themselves, and we didn't feel very kindly disposed towards
any Russians, as it was shortly after the mutiny of the
Slavo-British Legion at Troitsa. However, after we
had settled down a bit and had managed to draw our
rum ration, they thawed somewhat and became quite
affable, and presumably concluded that we were quite
harmless creatures with kind and generous faces,
though a trifle mad.

" Within a month or so they picked up quite a fair
knowledge of the English tongue, and blossomed out
with such words as ' Hiyah,' ' Sleepum,' ' Shovofski,'
' Rum,' ' Gin,' ' Goddam,' ' Bloffine,' and one or two
others. We, of course, had the pull over them, as we
had ' Dobra,' with ' Niet ' and ' Orchin ' to juggle with.

" Amongst our neighbours were the ' Niet Dobras,'
who owned an empty wooden house close to us from
which we frequently removed wood for our galley
fires. In order to stop this, Mrs. Niet Dobra boarded
in the spaces we had made in that side of the house
next to us, whilst she kept her eye on the doorway
which was on her side. This naturally did not hinder
us, and Mrs. N. D. is probably still fuming and wonder-

ing how her wood continued to vanish without anybody using the door.

"Mrs. Dobra was very partial to rum and gin, and we often used to give her a tot or two, for which she would get her eldest daughter, Anna, to do some of our washing. One evening she blew into the mess during dinner, just as we had come to the end of some plum duff, and was given about three fingers of gin in a cup, but the good old soul wouldn't drink it unless her host had an equal tot, which he did ; but we understand that he prefers it at ' bitters time ' and with a drop of water.

"Our C.O. was a noisy sort of a cove, and had the job of blowing up monitors that couldn't get down river on account of their deep draught, and other demolition jobs. T.N.T. bombs were dismantled and used, in conjunction with other explosives, for this, the empty brass sticks being thrown away into the refuse pit. Now, the refuse pit was a favourite haunt of the village urchins, who got a certain amount of nourishment from empty Maconochie tins and suchlike, and great was their joy when they discovered these brass tubes, which they sucked all day long despite our antics, gesticulations, and bad language.

"Eventually we got an interpreter to tell Mrs. D. that T.N.T., though sweet to taste, wasn't really a good diet in the long-run. Mrs. D., who had Metia, her youngest infant, in her arms, went into her room and produced a perfectly good Stokes bomb detonator and instantaneous fuze, which she said Metia had been sucking, and was that also poor diet ?

" One of the great social events of Malaya Zinovic-
vskaya was the '*malinky*' handicap races. All the
youth and beauty were rounded up, fallen in, and handi-
capped according to size, and then raced for chocolates.
These races were very popular, as everyone got prizes
sooner or later. On one occasion we raced the '*barishynas*,' and the winner, a beautiful fairy of some
20 odd stone or thereabouts, threw her arms around the
officer—a confirmed misogynist, by the way—who was
stationed at the finish with a box of chocolates.

" A good many of us were very keen on getting hold
of Russian needlework, embroidery, and the like, and
a few such things were picked up ; but the pick of the
bunch were the shawls, bed-covers, dresses, and various
bits of embroidery that Mrs. Dobra had made herself
for Anna, her eldest daughter. This, as Mrs. Dobra
explained, comprised Anna's trousseau, and therefore
she couldn't possibly give away separate pieces of it,
but that if one of us would only marry Anna, then we
could have the lot.

" We didn't have the time or opportunity to do any
shooting, but a good deal of slaughter was done
amongst the cockroaches with which Dobra-Ville
abounded. These insects live and multiply in the
cracks of the beams in summer, but die off in the
winter. The peasants, when the extreme cold begins
to set in, leave all the doors and windows of their
houses open for a couple of days or so, what time they
put up at their neighbours. This effectually kills all
the cockroaches until the summer comes again.

" The best time for a cocker hunt was in the evening,

when they came out of their cracks in swarms. Various methods of attack were used ; some used to go round with a hatchet, others with candles dropping grease on them, but the best method was to squirt neat Lysol into the cracks with a bilge squirt ; failing Lysol, Pyrene was a good substitute. When the hunting was good, one man with a bilge squirt would get a bag of about a hundred in ten minutes."

There was once an observation balloon. Always it swung above our heads through the twenty-four hours of the day. Sometimes there was an observer in the basket, more often not. The cinema operator once made it his home for a few hours. Kite Balloon barge was moored near Sea Plane Island, and one warm August morning there was an appalling revelation. The sausage still swung in the air, glittering in the brilliant sunshine. But on the yellow sands of Sea Plane Island lay a baby balloon. Rumour spread around the force. The marriage of a famous English beauty was as nothing to the stir caused by the fecundity of the hitherto respected observation balloon.

But worse was to follow. The next dawn another one had appeared. As the balloon had not descended to earth during the night, it was manifest that this latest creation had dropped from the skies.

The third morning dawned. Another balloon child.

The fourth morning. Another.

The fifth morning. Yet another.

Then the productivity of the balloon ceased. Perhaps it was as well. The strain was growing intoler-

able.   The climax came when the mother of the babes
collapsed one day on Sea Plane Beach, but even to her,
after her arduous labours, there came a resurrection—
but it cost the lives of all her children—and we knew
them no more.

CHAPTER III

HOW WE WON A GREAT BATTLE.

THE original plan of the Russian Relief Force had been most clearly defined. Granted favourable circumstances and attendant good luck, it was proposed, in co-operation with the naval flotilla, to make a lightning advance down the Dvina River as far as Kotlas, effect a junction with the then victorious armies of Admiral Koltchak, hand over the northern line to the Russians, start them on a combined movement towards Petrograd, and then to evacuate via Archangel ere the freezing up of that port. We had entertained, whilst training in England, visions of seeing Petrograd and even Moscow. One month of the Dvina saw the demise of all those dreams. The scheme as enumerated above was admittedly an ambitious one, requiring no small amount of dash and vigour on the part of both of His Majesty's services, as Kotlas is some 450 miles from Archangel.

Three main factors contributed to the abandonment of the plan—Koltchak's failure, the Russian troops, and the sudden outcry in the British Press for an immediate withdrawal. Experience has shown that the Russian troops rarely, if ever, conserve all the advantages they gain in a successful attack. Once the enemy is routed, the pursuit begins, according to all precepts of war. But there must come a stage when the advance goes beyond the limit of supplies, unless the services responsible are amazingly rapid.

The Russians in a successful attack invariably over-stepped the mark, exhausted themselves, ran out of supplies, and, on account of the distances covered by the operations, placed their lines of communication in jeopardy. Then the enemy, falling back on his bases and able to bring fresh troops into action, not only checked any further progress, but began to recover lost ground. Koltchak retreated rapidly, and all hopes of reaching Kotlas vanished.

At the same time strong pressure was being exercised through certain channels in England for an immediate withdrawal of all troops from North Russia. Evacuation in the face of the enemy, particularly when the enemy is cognizant of the movement, is a difficult proceeding.

Armchair critics—and there were many such in England at that time—fail to realize the terrific responsibilities involved in bringing away troops from a theatre of operations in face of the enemy.

If the demagogues, who at this period were shrieking " Evacuate Russia " to the Government of the country had even for twenty-four hours been present on the Dvina, it is possible that, despite all their stubbornness and ignorance, they might have realized the difficulties of the situation, and possibly the folly of leaving North Russia to herself.

In addition to these reasons, however, there were others more immediately concerning the forces engaged on the river. The enemy had laid considerable minefields. The absence of rise and fall of tide made sweeping a particularly dangerous operation. Heavy losses had already been incurred in clearing the river from Tulgas to Troitsa, and the operation had extended over seven days.

Behind the enemy's minefields lay his flotilla. He had not suffered greatly, and having no mines to deal with, his way of retreat was free. On the British side there was no railway. The river was amazingly low, and transport by water could not be relied upon. Roads were bad, bridges unequal to the stream of heavy artillery, and teams of heavy horses did not exist.

All these difficulties made the prospect of a rapid advance doubtful. In withdrawing, other equally important factors had to be considered. Hundreds of loyal Russians had been living in the security of the British protection for many months. To leave them to their probable fate on our evacuation was unthinkable. It was proposed (and eventually arranged) to give them an opportunity of leaving the country first, and to this end shipping and river transport had to be collected and utilized. The condition of the river militated against this work to a great degree. Finally, it became necessary to evolve a very extensive plan for evacuation, the first move in which came into operation on August 10th.

It was vital to strike a blow at the enemy's forces opposing us. There was much comment and criticism in the Press as to whether this blow was or was not offensive action and nothing else. In order to obtain freedom of movement for an operation so delicate as a complete evacuation, it was necessary seriously to cripple the enemy's fighting force. That was done.

The mining of the river, in order to obstruct and delay appreciably the subsequent advance of the Bolo flotilla, was necessary, particularly as it would enable as many ships of the British flotilla to get down the river as soon as the depth of water permitted.

The question of the Russian troops who would remain and, it was hoped, safeguard Archangel was not lost sight of. Elaborate plans for the holding of successive lines were drawn up.

These, therefore, were the problems confronting us at the commencement of August. The plans for a complete evacuation having been adopted, the details were carefully worked out, and the first stage, that of an offensive, culminated on August 10th in a most amazing victory for the British and Russian arms.

The first event that really happened to convince everyone of the possibility of an attack was the formation of the Trinity of Sectors. No. 1 Sector was the left bank ; No. 2, the naval forces ; and No. 3, the right bank. Written in plain English, it all looks very simple, but in reality it was most complex. In order to provide Sector Commanders, the two officers in command of the 45th and 46th Royal Fusiliers were made O.Cs. Nos. 1 and 3 respectively, and the Seconds-in-Command of each battalion manfully carried on. But O.Cs. of sectors must have adjutants and staff captains, and telephones and orderlies, and offices and maps, and Army Forms and pencils and pens. Eventually on each bank a miniature G.H.Q. was formed with all its attendant paraphernalia. The difficulty then arose as to where the sector finished and where the infantry battalions began. The elements contained in the sector commands, apart from the infantry, were very small. Complete disassociation from the infantry was therefore impossible, and many weary days were spent discovering which command should deal with this form and which command with that.

It all worked out easily, however, for after yards of official correspondence one sector adjutant dashed into the battalion adjutant with a polite query as to why the —— he didn't deal with it; and after a five-minute word battle normality reigned again, and the work of the Army progressed.

A new game was introduced at this period—ciphers. It was most fascinating for those who played it correctly. Brigade Headquarters blossomed out into a Cipher Officer, complete with subordinates and an office. Elaborate codes, calculated to puzzle even the most brilliant of Bolsheviks, were circulated amongst all and sundry. Figure codes are all very well in their way, but unfortunately army signallers have a strongly developed penchant for writing 8's like 0's, and 7's like 4's.

In the *sanctum sanctorum sanctissimi* of the cipher office long messages would be coded and sent buzzing forth on all the wires to the three sector officers. They were invariably labelled " URGENT—PRIORITY." Even the most hardened of adjutants winces a little at that superscription. When the message is delivered by a breathless orderly at 8.80 a.m., as most of the cipher messages seemed to be, the wincing becomes almost an attack of ague. With grim faces and set teeth, and hands tightly gripping a pink message form, sector adjutants could often be seen at dawn, with their pyjamas half hidden beneath British warms and gum-boots, wending their way to their quiet offices, there to elucidate the mystery of the " URGENT—PRIORITY."

One would imagine that difficulties now vanished. On the contrary, they increased. There happened to be two ciphers, and one never knew which was in operation. Therefore from the following—

75003   65298   17326   85943

would be produced something like this—

OFTRR   SMEZT   XOPHA   MNMLL,

which, of course, one immediately comprehended ; so the other code was tried with a similarly intelligible result.

Exasperation invariably led the puzzled decoder to utilize the telephone, with these results. Half an hour's delay in getting connected.

" Is that Brigade H.Q. ?"

" Yes."

" No. —— Sector speaking. I want the Cipher Officer."

" He's in bed."

" Can you send for him ?"

" It's a long way."

" Yes, but it is important. Send for him at once. It is about a cipher message."

Another hour or so passes, while the wretched sector officer waits in his solitary office. Then a buzz.

" Hullo, is that the —— Sector ?"

" Yes."

" Well, the Cipher Officer says if it is about that message sent out last night, it doesn't matter. It's not important. The morning will do. Ring up in the morning, and he will give you the message in clear."

Is it any wonder that even sector officers at times used bad language ? But there ! it deceived the Bolo, and that was the chief thing.

To thoroughly appreciate the formulation of the plan of attack, one must digress a little and describe the actual position of the opposing forces. The Bolos were holding a line astride the Dvina. It was well entrenched and heavily wired with substantial knife rests. Here and there in most advantageous positions he had strong blockhouses, built of logs, which were ever and always of the greatest nuisance. On the right bank he held the south bank of the Selmenga River, and on the left bank his line ran in front of Nijni Seltso. The flanks of the position extended into the forest about two miles on either side of the river. In depth the position stretched back on the right bank as far as Ivanovskaya, on the left to the Kodema River, about ten miles in each case. On the former bank the villages running in order from the front to the rear were Selmenga, Gorodok, and Borok, and Ivanovskaya ; and on the latter bank, Nijni Seltso, Sludka, Lipovets, and Chudinova, and finally Puchega.

The enemy strength was approximately 6,000 officers and men, 18 guns, and plenty of trench mortars and machine guns. In addition, he had his naval flotilla with all its guns. Our forces were considerably less. The G.O.C. had under his command at the inception of the attack 2 British infantry battalions (45th and 46th Royal Fusiliers), neither up to strength, 2 machine-gun companies (201st Machine Gun Company), 1 R.E. company (385th Field Company), and 1 Russian Brigade, less 1 battalion. The Russian battalion strength was approximately 300 bayonets.

Of guns there were thirteen 18-pounders, one 18-pounder (Mark IV), four 4·5 howitzers, two 15·5 mm. howitzers, two 60-pounders (manned by seamen), and one section 3·7 Mountain Artillery.

It was intended to utilize the services of the Russian cavalry and two more sections of the 3·7 Mountain Artillery, but the state of the ground in their sphere of operations was so bad that it rendered them useless.

The plan of attack on land after many discussions devolved into a very deep flanking movement on each bank of the river. The only question that arose was the feasibility of the infantry being able to march round the Bolo flank. The maps issued to the force generally ignored all features of the ground. The huge Selmenga forest was not shown at all. Maps of large scale and accuracy had therefore to be constructed, and elaborate reconnaissance had to be made round the enemy's flanks and behind his lines. The success of the patrols was amazing. Russian peasants who had spent their lives in the forest and knew every

track and footpath were brought into service. Dressed
in British uniform, they looked most awkward and
incongruous, yet they were wonderful guides. Led
by these men, small British patrols penetrated miles
behind the Bolo lines ; and when all the information
was collated, and added to the very valuable material
gained by Major Straker, the Chief Intelligence Officer,
maps of absolute accuracy were drawn, and it was upon
these made-at-home maps that the whole action was
fought.

There was terrific apprehension on the right bank
when Sergeant Whammond, M.C., and some of his patrol
failed to return after having been spotted from the
Bolo flank and fired upon. But the sergeant was too
old a hand in the bush game to get lost at such a
mere trifle, and he rolled up with his men two days
after, a little grubby and unshaven, but with a happy
smile and a notebook full of most wonderful information.

For his patrol work he subsequently received the
award of the M.M. and D.C.M., and no one in the
force deserved a decoration more than he did.

Efforts were also made to mystify the Bolo's intelligence department by sending British troops to work
on forest roads miles away from the forward zone.
In this connection a humorous story is told of the
march from Troitsa to Verknaya Reka of " D " Company of the 46th Royal Fusiliers.

A detachment of gunners accompanied the infantry.
Whatever the peaceable folk of the village imagined
our plans to be no one ever discovered, though they

CAPT. EDWARD ALTHAM, C.B., Royal Navy,
Who commanded the Naval Flotilla on the Dvina.

were sagacious enough to make the troops comfortable in billets and not to profiteer on eggs. At one of the halts on the way out a weary gunner flung down his equipment on the hind-legs of his mule. The animal immediately let out, as mules sometimes do. With great suddenness, the gunner was flung some yards by the kick he received, and finally landed in a sitting position on the other side of the road.

He gazed at the now quiescent mule in a half-apologetic manner.

" You —— ! It's a pity they didn't fit you with Phillips's military rubber heels," he said, and then fainted. It required two water-bottles of what was at that time precious fluid to bring him back to consciousness.

Transport ! Transport ! Transport ! Such was the perpetual cry on the days immediately preceding zero. Someone truly remarked that the entire Dvina force had gone "drosky mad." Never before in the history of North Russia has there ever been such a collection of droskies, drivers, and ponies. The official account of the D.A.D.S. and T. is worth giving here :—

" To obtain this transport," he says, " compulsory hiring of all transport was ordered from all villages on both banks of the river from Prilotski on the north bank and Navolok on the south.

" The requisitioning parties left Beresnik on the morning of August 6th, and by the morning of August 8th the transport began coming in rapidly at the rendezvous Topsa Church and the village of Zarvadie for north and south banks respectively.

" On August 7th, being " Y " day, all the transport in Topsa and Yako parishes was requisitioned.

" The total number of horses available (after return- ing sick and young horses) by the compulsory hiring was just over 1,100, which was distributed roughly 900 to units, and with the balance I established a pool of 100 on either bank to guard against any unforeseen demands.

" No payment in money was made for this transport ; each peasant was given

$$1 \text{ funt of flour,}$$
$$\tfrac{1}{4} \text{ ,, sugar,}$$
$$\tfrac{1}{28} \text{ ,, tea,}$$

for every day worked with the force, the period reckon- ing from the day of leaving their village to the day of return. The peasants appeared to be quite satisfied with this payment in kind."

But official reports give little idea of the humour and possibly the tragic side of this great concourse of droskies. Whole families, almost generations, of drivers arrived. Old bearded men and wizened old women, their sons and daughters in the prime of life, their grandchildren in their teens—all rolled up with their droskies. And such droskies ! Old ones, decrepit from age, held together by string and wire ; new ones glistening in the sunshine from fresh paint ; droskies that creaked as they moved, and others that just fell to pieces.

There was not one that had not half its capacity

occupied by a sack of feed. The driver filled almost the remaining portion of space, so that its load was limited. The extent of the conversation between the British and the drivers was " *Scurry and Scoffem* " on the Russian side, and on the other side " *Dobra and Kharasho.*"

There they were, four or five hundred of them, horses, carts, and drivers, crammed into an open space behind Brigade Headquarters. Weather conditions hardly improved the state of the assembled multitude, for rain fell heavily during their congregation. But their imperturbable natures were unaffected by rain. The wise ones merely retreated into the marquee provided for them, and the foolish ones remained outside, paring and eating the inevitable raw turnip, and getting wet. Reasons for this gathering of droskies did not bother them very much. Poor simple creatures as they were, all they knew was that they had been ordered to come for the armies. It was the war, and in war they must expect anything. If they had happened to be in Bolshevik territory, it would have been the same, except, perhaps, they might not have been paid in precious food. Still, " *Nichevo.*"

Finally they were all assembled, and eventually in pouring rain despatched to the areas of concentration, there to undergo the most trying of all experiences.

Rain and the opening of a British offensive seem to be synonymous terms. Their amalgamation is traceable to the early days of warfare in Belgium. Ypres witnessed many attacks, it seemed always in the rain. One always expected it to rain the morning before zero, and to continue till one was relieved after the attack was over and the Boche line won. Surprise and annoyance, therefore, were tempered by familiarity when it began to rain a few days before zero day on the Dvina. It was the surest indication of the proximity of a British attack.

Living in a forest, beneath a rude shelter of branches, twigs and leaves, has its advantages when all is fair, but during heavy and consistent rain it leaves much to be desired. Zero minus one day was a terrible strain for everyone. It poured unceasingly, and the mud squelched higher and higher round one's ankles. By the evening the whole of the assembled force was thoroughly wet through.

Groups of men huddled round miserable smoky fires, voicing their contempt of Russia, rain, wet clothes, soaked biscuits, damp small-arms ammunition, war, Bolos—anything and everything.

The day had been occupied in issuing battle rations, extra small-arms ammunition, picks, shovels, Véry lights, S O S rockets, bombs, and all the paraphernalia the unfortunate soldier has to carry into a well-formed battle. The only things not carried were mosquito nets and their rings.

On both banks of the river at the point of concentration these scenes were enacted. The Bolshevik was in blissful ignorance of these preparations. Bombing and shelling of his guns and headquarters had been stopped a fortnight previously. A desultory shell was sent over occasionally, but the general impression amongst the Bolos at this period was that we were

hastily packing up our goods and chattels, prepara-
tory to running away and leaving the whole country
to their tender mercies. Alas ! they were the more
deceived. The Russian troops were concentrated
from Morjegerskaya under cover of darkness, and only
brought up to the forward area at the last moment.

There were three separate columns of troops on each
bank, each with a separate objective, though the whole
attack was to commence at a given hour—12 noon
on August 10th. Each column was self-contained.
Everyone had wireless and signal arrangements completed. On the left bank (No. 1 Sector) there was the
Seltso column (Captain G. C. de Mattos, M.C.), whose
objective was the Bolo positions at Seltso and Nijni
Seltso ; the Sludka-Lipovets column (Major S. G. F.
Shepherd, M.C.), to capture the two villages named ;
and the Chudinova column (Captain F. G. Cavendish,
M.C.).

On the right bank (No. 3 Sector), commanded by
Lieut.-Colonel H. H. Jenkins, D.S.O., the columns
were—the Selmenga column (Captain Wass, M.C.),
whose object was to carry out a holding attack in rear
of the Bolo front line ; the Gorodok column (Major
A. E. Percival, D.S.O., M.C.) ; and the Borok column
(Major Nightingale, M.C.).

Then the Navy (No. 2 Sector) was all in readiness
also to take its part in the action. They had a taste
of the battle before anyone else. In the afternoon
of the 9th H.M. " M. 33 " was at anchor in the " advanced position," and was lying there in readiness
for anything that might come along, when the Bolos

opened fire on her with two 4·2-inch guns mounted on the Selmenga Road. Their shooting was watched with some interest, as, although they were putting their shells rather wide of the mark at first, they were obviously getting nearer to their target.

Their observation was so good that in a few minutes they had hit " M. 33," who immediately started to get under way for the purpose of moving out of the line of fire. She managed to do this all right, but not until she had been hit again by a shot which caused damage, necessitating her retirement to the flotilla anchorage.

She was relieved in her duties by another Monitor, which went up and anchored in the position where the Bolos had been making such good target practice ; but the Bolo seemed to have satisfied himself with having registered accurately on the spot, or perhaps our sea-planes had begun to attend to them too closely ! Suffice it to say that the new arrival in the " advanced position " was allowed to lie undisturbed by any war-like demonstrations on the part of the enemy.

At about 3 a.m. on August 10th the ship's company of the " duty " ship was awakened from a peaceful sleep by the explosion of an enemy shell which, coming out of the fog which had settled down, had fallen about 15 yards from the captain's cabin. This was followed shortly by another shell, which fell 5 yards away. Then ensued a somewhat hot bombardment, in which the enemy shells fell literally all round the ship, missing her by mere inches.

This was getting too warm for the bravest, and so

the ship got under way and trundled up river to a spot rather nearer the enemy, but hidden from him by the bank of fog, whence she could observe the continued and accurate shooting of the enemy on to the spot where she had been laying, until the fog lifted and the enemy discovered that he had been expending his ammunition on the surface of the river.

The only chance of success for the land forces was the element of complete surprise. If we could successfully move around the flanks and concentrate without the enemy's knowledge, then success was assured. On the enemy's left flank (No. 1 Sector) a very lengthy approach march had to be faced. So long was it that the columns had to commence it on August 8th. At six o'clock in the evening, therefore, the columns moved off from Yakolevskoe, and the following day at noon, after having rested, an advanced guard was sent on to cover the R.E. section, who had been given the task of improving the forest tracks, so as to make it passable for pack animals.

The remainder of the column left their halting-place (2nd Mill) at four in the afternoon of the 8th, and proceeded with the march. On the morning of " Y " day a Bolo deserter was brought in by the outposts. To the jubilation of everyone, he said that the enemy knew absolutely nothing of the turning movement actually in operation, or of any attack being contemplated by us. Marching on " Y " day was a great strain for all the troops. Tracks were almost impassable. Most of the loads of the pack animals had to be man-handled for considerable distances.

An officers' patrol (Captain Henderson, Lieut. Penson, and two other ranks) investigated the country south-west of Sludka, with the object of deploying Major Shepherd's column for attack. They found a sad state of affairs. The forward track was extremely marshy, and in all probability troops would not be able to cross—certainly not pack animals. As the 8·7 mountain guns were being carried in this fashion, the report was far from pleasing. The more everyone saw of the ground, the greater became the depression. Nevertheless the forming up positions were finally reached by all the columns on the left bank, though everyone was wet through, tired out, and not too happy.

The columns on the right bank had neither the formidable march nor the insurmountable difficulties of their comrades to face. The march did not begin till nine o'clock on the night of the 9th, and the only real obstacle was the Selmenga River, which had to be forded. The approach to the river was down a very steep bank. Swamps were bad, and the pace was therefore exceedingly slow. The fording of the river for the leading troops was simple and not at all un-pleasant. But half-way through the column the ford was much deeper as the result of many hundreds of feet passing over it. So deep did it finally become that the Russians wanted to remove their boots and socks, and coercive measures had to be applied before they would dash across. But after four hours of con-siderable apprehension, for the noise of crossing seemed terrific, the whole force had passed over, and moved on towards the forming up positions.

On the approach march no sign had been seen
of the enemy, but one could hear his guns, which
were busy firing into our defences at Selmenga,
in total ignorance that we were behind him. All
that now could be done for the next few hours
was to rest and keep the force concealed as much
as possible. All ranks and animals badly needed
this rest, as they had been marching for eight hours,
and it had been impossible to off-load the pack animals
en route. All column commanders, tired as they undoubtedly were, took the opportunity to reconnoitre in
front of them, with a view to selecting their assembly
positions. By 11 a.m. all columns were in their
assembly positions.

All things considered, the assembly of the troops
was a marvellous operation. To pass completely round
the two flanks of the enemy, without even arousing
the slightest suspicion, was an amazing feat. Tribute
must be paid to the discipline of all ranks. Smoking
was prohibited for some considerable time, talking was
discouraged, and fires were forbidden. Everyone was
wet through, yet spirits were high ; and, as one of the
sector commanders wrote after the battle, " all difficulties were overcome by the splendid keenness of all
ranks, whose one object was to have a good show."

During the night a slow mustard gas shell bombardment of the Selmenga defences was indulged in, with
an occasional tear gas shell thrown in. The Bolo had
not had the interesting experience of gas up till then,
and, having only a very poor respirator, he suffered
considerably.

So at 12 noon on the 10th the attack began. In dealing generally with the attack, it is simpler to narrate the events and then deal with the action in each sector separately. Events therefore transpired as follows :—

1245 hours.—Report from Russians that Nijni Seltso had been captured. This was incorrect.

1320 hours.—Report from O.C. " I " Sector that Kotchinka and Chudinova were captured. Major Shepherd's column was advancing on Sludka.

1348 hours.—Artillery fire called for on Borok (No. 3 Sector), and this was given by H.M.S. *Humber*.

1414 hours.—First objective at Borok captured.

1450 hours.—Column Commander Seltso attack reports " attack on Seltso repulsed, and am reorganizing."

1458 hours.—Gorodok reported captured, with many prisoners and guns.

1500 hours.—New attack on Seltso ordered by G.O.C. for 1820 hours.

1539 hours.—Artillery fire asked for on Borok. Given by naval guns. Selmenga column reports enemy still in front line.

1600 hours.—Concentrated bombardment of Selmenga defences.

1800 hours.—Nijni Seltso still in Bolo hands. Hurricane bombardment opened upon it.

1915 hours.—Enemy fled from Seltso, surrendering in large numbers. Pursuit was pushed vigorously.

2200 hours.—Enemy holding Selmenga defences
counter-attacked Gorodok; attack repulsed;
400 enemy killed and captured.
2302 hours.—Borok captured, with 80 prisoners.

Such was the bald outline of the first day's action
ending at midnight. It was not known till three in the
morning that Sludka and Lipovets had also been
captured, though the O.C. No. 1 Sector, Colonel
Davies, D.S.O., and some of his staff were missing.

This amazing victory can only be appreciated by
dealing with the definite actions in each sector, and
that I propose to do at once.

THE NAVY.

The naval flotilla, as keen as any 1914 volunteer to
take part in a real battle, commenced serious work
on the Bolo defences at 20 minutes past 11 on zero
morning.

H.M.S.'s *Humber*, M.27, M.31, and M.33 were engaged. Seaplanes assisted in bombing and spotting.
The kite balloon, working from its barge, was moved
up close to the ships to assist in spotting and reconnaissance.

H.M.S.'s *Humber* and *Cicala* devoted special attention to the enemy gunboats. So effective was the fire
that the Bolos turned tail and fled. The gunboat
disappeared from view with a heavy list, a matter for
much jubilation amongst the British gunnery men.

Coastal motor boats were busily watching for any
possible chance to help, and when a party was spotted

on the left bank the tiny craft tore up river and dispersed the already nervous Bolos with their Lewis gun fire.

When trouble was announced at Borok, the Navy soon set to work and banged shell after shell into the village. The result of that shoot was exceedingly beneficial to the infantry, who were not having too pleasant a time in front of Borok. All through the afternoon the guns of the Navy dropped shells on to points selected for special treatment. They enjoyed the hurricane bombardment of Seltso amazingly.

H.M.S.'s *Humber*, M.27, and M.33 bombarded in conjunction with the shore artillery, and Nijni Seltso was taken. Subsequently fire was lifted 500 yards and another 37 minutes' bombardment carried out, the latter part being very intensive. Seltso was taken that evening.

As one naval officer described it, " A pleasing sight was to see Seltso on fire, the whole sky glowing a beautiful red. I suppose this was an everyday sight to the Army, but I must confess it impressed us vastly, as it seemed such a fitting climax."

But the Navy's work did not end with mere shooting. The coastal motor boats had another little adventure when the attack on Seltso took place, and their Lewis guns did good work amongst the fleeing Bolos.

During these operations the flotilla also co-operated with the Army ashore.

Thirty-five seamen under Lieutenant M. S. Spalding, R.N., and thirty-nine Marines under Lieutenant C. M. Sergeant, R.M.L.I., were landed to reinforce at the base.

Twenty seamen under Lieutenant R. P. Martin, R.N., manned two 60-pounders, one of which had been rescued from the bottom of the river. The 60-pounders were actively employed during the bombardments ; the marines subsequently assisted to garrison Seltso, and the seamen were at Yakolevskoe.

An extensive enemy minefield was discovered off Seltso, and a passage cleared for transport up to Nijni Seltso. While sweeping this, one of the steamboats was mined and Lieutenant C. E. McLaughlin, R.N., was killed. This officer, with the late Lieutenant Fitzherbert-Brockholes, R.N., had been employed in the advanced mine-sweeping steamboats on every occasion, and had rendered very gallant service. In view of the fact that no farther advance was intended, mine-sweeping was stopped, as the risk outweighed the convenience of water transport.

The enemy's mines precluded sending minelaying craft above Seltso, but fifteen small " whisker " mines which the enemy had floated down river were caught and prepared for service, taken up by road on country carts, and laid in the river off Lipovets. Subsequently eight small horned mines were pulled out of the enemy minefield, and similarly transported and laid at night above Puchega.

These lines effectively prevented the enemy ships coming down and attacking our base at Troitsa during the evacuation and after our own ships withdrew.

The work was carried out with much enterprise and ability under Lieutenant-Commander (T.) Arthur J. L. Murray, O.B.E., R.N., who was, unfortunately,

njured subsequently by the premature explosion of a
mine pistol while rendering an enemy mine safe.

Seaplanes did not have such a happy time. Mist
and rain interfered considerably with their operations.
So bad were the conditions on " Y " day that no flights
were possible. On the morning of the 10th one Short
seaplane crashed near Topsa, but fortunately the pilot
and observer were unhurt. It was all due to having
lost their way in the mist. Nevertheless, the spotting
for the flotilla proved of some service, though it was
tricky work. The old friend, the observation balloon,
held its head high all the time. It was useful in giving
early information of enemy movements.

It was also a most effective guide to a party which
had lost its way in the forest subsequent to the operations of August 10th, and was lit up by searchlight at
night for this purpose.

Naval observation positions were established on
both banks, as near the front line as possible, and connected by telephone with the S.N.O.R. and Battalion
Headquarters. They were of the utmost value in
keeping the flotilla informed of the position of our front
line, enemy movements, and for spotting. They frequently came under very heavy fire on being located
by the enemy.

The Left Bank.

The attack on the left bank was a prolonged one.
The Bolo put up a strong resistance in some quarters,
and the Seltso column had a bad time at first, though,
as we have seen, they later captured the town.

Marshes and swamps had effectively held up all the mountain artillery and cavalry, and the infantry themselves were very tired when the attack opened at noon. The Seltso column at that time was 500 yards southeast of its objective.

An ill fate awaited the column commander, Captain G. C. de Mattos, for within a few minutes of the launching of the attack he was killed, and the command devolved on Captain H. L. Sumner, of the Light Trench Mortar Battery. A heavy and an accurate fire was poured into the British troops from machine guns in blockhouses, and rifles in the Bolshevik entrenchments. The position was such that Captain Sumner, when he took command, deemed it advisable—and wisely so—to withdraw, reorganize, and attack again. The enemy even had the temerity to launch a strong counter-attack, which hardly improved the position of the Seltso column. The G.O.C., having become possessed of this knowledge, realized that the column was unable to reach its objective, owing to its having been severely handled, and, as the element of surprise no longer existed, he ordered the commander of this column to reorganize and get in touch with Colonel Davies, O.C. No. 1 Sector, and not to attempt another attack. Meanwhile, he ordered from the reserve the remainder of the battalion (one company of which had failed to take Nijni Seltso) into a position of readiness north and south of Nijni Seltso.

It was impressed upon everyone the necessity of capturing Nijni Seltso, and the new attack was launched at 1820 hours.

Guns of all calibres on both banks, all machine guns, and every available gun the ships could bring to bear, opened up a hurricane bombardment on Nijni Seltso, from 1800 hours to 1820 hours. The whole of the guns lifted 500 yards at 1820 hours, and fired a protection barrage until 1900 hours.

Many fires were started in Seltso and the enemy's defences, and blockhouses were frequently hit.

The enemy opened a brisk machine gun and rifle fire against the attacking infantry, and the attack appeared hung up. At 1850 hours the O.P. Officer at Brigade Command Post reported the enemy retiring from Nijni Seltso. The guns lengthened range 300 yards ; the guns of the ships were fired on the exits of Seltso ; machine guns were switched so as to cut off retreat. The reserve was ordered to pursue. The response to this order was rapid. The enemy at once ceased fighting, and surrendered in large numbers, many fleeing into the woods, large bodies making for the foreshore, where they came under fire from the machine guns on the island north of Seltso. The pursuit was pushed vigorously with the reserve and a battery of artillery.

Thus Seltso fell into our hands. But it was not taken without heavy losses on our side, from the column commander downwards. Many officers and men, however, distinguished themselves, and a few of the awards are worthy of special notice.

In face of heavy fire, No. 130153 Private J. Hunter, of the 45th Royal Fusiliers, manœuvred his Lewis gun into position. He was wounded while doing so. Un-

LIEUT.-COL. H. H. JENKINS, D.S.O.

The Genial Commander of the 46th Bn.
Royal Fusiliers.

LIEUT.-COL. C. S. DAVIES, D.S.O.

The Leicestershire Regiment,
Who Commanded the 45th Bn. Royal Fusiliers.

daunted by this, he continued at duty, opened fire
on the enemy, and continued firing till his gun was
hit and put out of action. He then secured an abandoned enemy gun and fired that till he was ordered
to withdraw. Hunter was subsequently awarded the
Distinguished Conduct Medal for his gallant action.

Another award in the Seltso fight was a bar to
the Military Cross conferred on Temporary-Lieutenant
Llewellyn Wynne Jones, M.C., Royal Welsh Fusiliers,
attached 45th Royal Fusiliers, for conspicuous gallantry
and devotion to duty during the attack. He per-
sonally scouted the defences prior to the attack, and
during the action, though in danger of being surrounded, he withdrew his men, bringing out all the
casualties.

A Distinguished Conduct Medal was also awarded
to 129534 Private R. Lees, 45th Royal Fusiliers, for
conspicuous gallantry and devotion to duty in bringing
back an abandoned Lewis gun under exceptionally
heavy rifle and machine-gun fire.

The Sludka-Lipovets column had much better luck.
Their first obstacle was the village of Kochimaka, but
the enemy did not show much fight, and it was soon
taken.

On arrival there, however, the troops were met with
heavy fire from the gunboats and barges at a range
of 300 to 500 yards. These were engaged with machine-
gun and rifle fire, and they hoisted the white flag.
Unfortunately, there were no boats to send out boarding parties, and after a few minutes all naval craft
again opened fire. Had only two field guns managed

H

to get across the marshes these gunboats and barges would have surrendered.

Ten minutes after zero this column had another two villages to its credit — Jitna and Kochamika. Here, at the latter place, they bagged a Bolo anti-aircraft gun. The village of Zaniskaya was the next to fall, and at 1.50 p.m., only two hours after zero, they triumphantly entered Sludka. But calamity descended even on this column, for ten minutes later the column commander, Major Shepherd, was killed on the main road in front of Zaniskaya.

It was a direct hit by a shell on the Column Head-quarters, and besides the O.C. eight other ranks were killed, and Captain Ficklin, G.H.Q. Liaison Officer, was wounded.

Major Mayne, 201st M.G.C., then assumed command of the column. Ficklin had an exciting time subse-quently, for, after having been convoyed through Sludka, he was thrown into the marshes by the Bolo stretcher-bearers, as were several other wounded, when Bolos from the wood opened fire on the wounded convoy. The Bolo stretcher-bearers then disappeared. The escorting Russian troops bolted, and escorting British formed a line on the river side of the marsh. After crawling about the woods, he eventually found the 45th Royal Fusiliers transport, who brought him in. Other wounded thrown into the marsh did the same.

The wood the whole of this time was full of unarmed Bolos and our Russians, the former surrendering, or trying to, and the latter refusing help and trying to escape.

The column then went hard at it for Lipovets, and at half-past four in the afternoon that town fell into our hands. The men of " A " Company, 45th Royal Fusiliers, were fortunate in discovering the Bolshevik commander of Lipovets in his headquarters, and both he and his staff were speedily despatched. Already over 580 prisoners had been taken, and more were drifting in as the minutes rolled by.

The column was now very short of ammunition, and, hearing that the attack on Seltso had failed, Major Mayne, the commander, held a conference of officers to decide on their plan of action. Eventually it was agreed not to attack Seltso, but to flank it by moving through forest paths to the 1st Mill. The men were practically exhausted, and had had no food that day, having sacrificed their rations for the purpose of carrying more ammunition.

Bolo prisoners brought in at this time confirmed the news that Seltso was strongly held, and the British guns could be heard bombarding it.

Leaving the Lipovets—Seltso road, the column, with all the wounded and prisoners, took to the forest tracks.

The Bolos in the forest attacked at 3.20 a.m., but were driven off by the rearguard, thus enabling the column to cross the river over a single plank bridge— a most difficult and dangerous operation.

The Bolo prisoners at this time made a general stampede, throwing away material which had been given them to carry.

The column then re-organized and moved to the

1st Mill, fighting hard the whole way. At 7 a.m. the whole column had reached its final position, but Seltso had finally fallen and the tumult had ceased.

Losses in men had been considerable in this column as well, particularly when the enemy gunboats fired on Zaniskaya after its capture. They did very great execution, as the bank here was 30 feet high, and our men had to get on top and be seen before they could take on the gunboats, which the men attempted to do with Lewis guns and trench mortars, but apparently without hurting them.

The chief award in this action was that of the Distinguished Service Order to Captain Harry Heaton, M.C., 19th Durham Light Infantry, attached 45th Royal Fusiliers :—

> " On August 10th, 1919, during attacks on Kochamika, Sludka, and Lipovets, he was commanding the battalion. He personally led his troops in all these attacks, and showed conspicuous gallantry and efficiency throughout under heavy fire, taking all objectives."

Great gallantry was also shown at that critical time by another of the 45th Royal Fusiliers officers, Lieutenant Harris Rendall, O.B.E., M.C., of the Royal Scots Fusiliers. He was subsequently given a well-deserved bar to his Military Cross.

The official story read thus :—

> " His skilful handling of his platoon was largely responsible for the gaining of all objectives. By opening fire on the enemy's river craft he saved

the column a large number of casualties. Two steamers and a gunboat put up the white flag."

Other bars to Military Crosses given that day were the two following :—

Lieutenant Robert Ramsay, M.C., 1st Royal Highlanders, attached 45th Royal Fusiliers :—

"For conspicuous gallantry and good leadership. He, as adjutant to the column, when his commanding officer was killed, took command until the next senior officer could be informed. He was practically cut off with the whole of Column Headquarters when the enemy landed a party of sailors. He managed to extricate headquarters and keep up constant communication with the forward attacking companies."

Lieutenant John Hubert Penson, M.C., Royal Engineers :—

"For conspicuous gallantry and devotion to duty on August 10th, 1919. He guided the Sludka-Lipovets Column for three days, and brought it to within 400 yards of the enemy's position unobserved. Again, on August 10th, the column, having decided to withdraw from Lipovets owing to shortage of ammunition, he guided it out under heavy fire."

The first officer to arrive in Sludka was Lieutenant Edward Leopold Sutro, 4th Royal Fusiliers, attached 45th Royal Fusiliers, who was awarded the Military Cross for gallantry and good work. He was in command of the leading platoon, and gained all his objectives. He moved on Sludka, and was the first officer to arrive there. He was largely instrumental in the capture of 350 prisoners.

Some of the Distinguished Conduct Medals awarded are also worthy of special notice. They included the following :—

129963 C.S.M. E. Almey, 45th Royal Fusiliers.

" For great gallantry and determination. He led a small party of men against a machine gun which was firing on the right flank of Sludka, and captured the gun with 50 prisoners."

129545 Private J. P. Mason, 45th Royal Fusiliers.

" For conspicuous gallantry and devotion to duty. On two occasions, whilst No. 1 of Lewis gun, he engaged enemy gunboats, and, although heavily shelled, he kept firing till he silenced the enemy fire."

133029 Private N. M. Brooke, 45th Royal Fusiliers.

" During the attack on Kochamika and Sludka, August 10th, 1919, he showed great gallantry and skill in ascertaining the enemy's positions, and under heavy fire came back with reliable information, enabling his platoon to advance without casualties. He materially contributed to the success of a difficult operation."

130228 Private H. L. Sharpe, 45th Royal Fusiliers.

" For conspicuous gallantry and devotion to duty on August 10th, 1919, in dressing and evacuating wounded under heavy rifle and machine-gun fire. He set a very fine example to those with him."

129173 Lance-Sergeant W. D. Fox, 45th Royal Fusiliers.

" For great pluck and devotion to duty on August 10th, 1919. He was in charge of a small party that became detached from the main body. He, with an officer, was in charge of 250 prisoners and some 20 men. For two and a half days this party was in the forest without food, and was being constantly harassed by the enemy."

43159 Corporal C. Kilby, 201st Machine Gun Corps.

" For great gallantry and good work on August 10th-11th, 1919. At Sludka on August 10th he covered the withdrawal of the machine guns to another position by remaining behind and sniping the enemy. At the Sheika crossing on August 11th he collected a party of men, formed a line on river bank, and covered the crossing of the remaining troops."

These few examples I have quoted are sufficient to show the spirit and determination of the troops, the spirit that always brings victory to the arms of Britain.

The Chudinova Column, in command of Captain Cavendish, M.C., succeeded in reaching its objective without the extreme trouble experienced by the other columns. His orders were to take the village and then join the reserve, and report to O.C. No. 1 Sector. He was wounded whilst doing do. These two companies of Russians remained in Chudinova for a short time, and then retired along the road they had come. The situation was, however, straightened out by other troops shortly afterwards.

The exciting feature of the action on the left bank was the loss of the Sector Commander, Colonel Davies, with some of his staff. The party was cut off by the enemy, who were moving from Kochamika to Sludka, and were unable to rejoin any column for the remainder of the operation.

They were only saved by the observation balloon. Their adventures were amazing. About 2.30 p.m. the Colonel decided to join Shepherd's column at Sludka. As they moved along the crest of the hill, under shrapnel fire from a Bolo gunboat, a column was seen to be leaving Kochamika. A runner was dispatched to discover their identity. They proved to be civilians evacuating. The O.C. and his party continued to move towards Sludka, when they bumped a party of Bolo Marines. The enemy allowed them to come within 50 yards before he opened fire with rifles and machine guns. But his fire was so erratic that no one was hit, though everybody disappeared with amazing alacrity. The party consisted of the Colonel, Captain Booth, Captain Knock (Chaplain to the 45th Royal Fusiliers), Lieutenant Penson, and two runners.

A council of war ensued, and much shouting in Russian being heard, Penson went forward to interpret it. He failed to return. In an effort to rejoin the force they had left, the small party marched north. They were fired on. So they went east. Fired on again. They went west, with the same cheerless result. Added to these pleasant interludes was the rain, which was now descending in torrents. Three privates of the North Russian Regiment then joined the party. They were also lost, and shortly after three Bolos surrendered. One of them volunteered to guide the party back to Yakolevskoe. The rough route was checked by the compass, but a huge marsh was encountered, and in the midst of it Bolo trench mortar shells commenced to descend.

About nine o'clock, tired out, wet through, hungry and desolate, the three officers decided to rest for the night on a small wooded island in the marsh. The Bolo prisoners, most anxious to please, soon produced a fire, and dried the socks of the three Britishers. One of the Russian soldiers also arrived with hot tea and biscuits. All through the night one officer was on watch—first the Colonel, then the padre, then Booth.

Rifle fire disturbed them at five o'clock in the morning. It continued at intervals, and so tracks were made for some high ground lying to the northwest. Once there, the firing broke out with renewed vigour, punctuated by shouting in Russian and cries in English of " Come on !"

Near midday a track was struck in which fresh hoofprints were visible and a telephone wire was in existence. The question was as to whether the evidences of life were British or Bolo. Going north along the track, blood-stained bandages and food were discovered. The Russians were convinced they were left by the

Bolos, and in proof of their contention a violent scurry ensued, both the prisoners and the Russians knocking over the officers and diving into the thick bush. Their only comment when they were gathered together again was " Plenty Bolo."

In the confusion the padre and three others were separated from Colonel Davies and Captain Booth. The former party were lucky, for they fell in with a small party of the 45th Royal Fusiliers. A party was at once sent out to discover Colonel Davies, but they were unsuccessful. Colonel Davies and his men were busy looking for the vanished padre, but neither found each other, and the chaplain eventually arrived at Yakolevskoe about ten o'clock on the night of the 11th.

The O.C., with Booth, one Bolo, and two Russians, moved in a north-westerly direction from the point where they had lost Knock. Advice in the words " Scurry ! scurry !" was freely given by one of the Russians ; but as the marsh was almost up to their knees, progress was limited to the rate of one mile per hour.

Dinner was served at half-past nine. It consisted of sweetened water and army biscuit. But rifle shots disturbed this meal also, and a hasty retreat was made from the welcome fire that had been set going. Darkness came down, and a halt for the night was called. Sleep was out of the question. It was raining heavily and was extremely cold. As soon as dawn came the weary men moved on into another huge marsh. But their trials were coming to an end. While struggling in the marsh, with eyes lifted to heaven, the Colonel spotted the observation balloon far off, swinging high in the grey sky.

" Booth, look at that !"

Captain Booth gurgled with joy, and took a bearing with indecent haste. So relieved were the wanderers that they sat down to breakfast. All they had left was water and biscuit, and that was the last of the food.

Booth then climbed a very tall tree, and succeeded in locating both Yakolevskoe and Troitsa, and tracks were made for the former village. The remaining small rivers were crossed in luxury—the tame Bolo carrying both officers over on his back. They had only one more exciting experience. A British naval sentry in the blockhouse line put a couple of shots close to them while they were walking wearily down the road to Yako. Their language soon convinced him they were British.

The jubilation at headquarters at the arrival home of the long lost sector commander and Booth can hardly be described. The Russian who had stayed with them joined in the celebrations by repeating continuously, " War finish, plenty scoffem." Needless to say, he was given vast quantities of food. Booth took the Bolo to the rear in a Ford car, much to his astonishment, which increased considerably when he was handed over to the prisoners' cage.

Amazing rumours had been current in the force as to the fate of the party. Colonel Davies had been reported killed, Booth wounded and, in company with

Knock, in the hands of the Bolos. The Intelligence Branch had even taken the precaution to wire G.H.Q. that they had plenty of Bolo Battalion Commanders and Commissars in the prison cage, ready for immediate exchange.

Thus the observation balloon, despite its somewhat shady past, proved the salvation of both Colonel Davies and Captain Booth. But it is dangerous to mention the word " marshes " to either of them.

THE RIGHT BANK.

The action in No. 3 Sector, commanded by Lieut.-Colonel H. H. Jenkins, D.S.O., was entirely successful. The ground, though very wet, was not so impassable, and the Bolshevik only showed real fight at the village of Borok.

The Selmenga column had to deliver a holding attack against the enemy dispositions in the forward defences, which ran down to the south bank of the Selmenga River. So successfully did Captain Wass, M.C., manœuvre his command into position, that one of his platoon commanders—a sturdy South African, Lieutenant Alex. Smith, D.C.M.—managed to creep within a few hundred yards of the Bolo field guns, and he had the indescribable pleasure of listening to the raucous commands of the battery commander (his subsequent victim), and hearing the crash of the gun firing on the trenches, in which the British no longer adopted a defensive attitude.

Despite the efforts of this column, however, the enemy managed to slip through the cordon, and succeeded in reaching Gorodok. Their fate on arriving there must be left to the narrative dealing with the operations of that column. Captain Wass contented himself with mopping up the forest, and found quite a few Bolos, all suffering from the effects of gas.

Tear gas troubled the enemy considerably. The prisoners were all affected by it, and in their lachrymose condition, they voiced bitter anguish, believing themselves to be blinded for life.

The Gorodok column, under Major A. E. Percival, D.S.O., M.C., had a wonderful time. They had attached to them two companies of the 1/3rd North Russian Regiment, under Captain Posnikoff, M.C. These Russians distinguished themselves, and brought forth the admiration of all the British troops engaged in the attack.

A close reconnaissance showed that there was a commanding ridge about halfway between the wood and the village, which would have to be the objective of the first bound, and the artillery and Stokes guns were detailed to fire on this ridge for five minutes to cover the advance. During the reconnaissance a Bolo sentry could be seen walking up and down the ridge about 300 yards from the British position.

Considerable difficulty was experienced by the right attack in finding a suitable joining-up ground, owing to the extremely marshy nature of the ground and the close proximity of a battery of enemy guns. By clever handling, however, Captain de Miremont, D.S.O., M.C., succeeded in getting his troops into position, and at zero hour (12 noon) all was in readiness for the attack.

The battery and Stokes guns fired well, one section of the latter succeeding in getting off forty rounds in a little over a minute, and the infantry could be seen moving forward to the ridge. The attack from this quarter was evidently a complete surprise, the sentries appearing to be too much taken aback to take any action, and little difficulty was experienced in capturing the first objective, though it was a strong position, well protected with wire and defended by machine guns.

With fine dash and no hesitation, both assaulting columns immediately moved on to the village, 500 yards distant, and so rapid was the advance that it was necessary to stop the artillery fire at zero plus five minutes. Several of the enemy put up a stout resistance in the village, especially towards the western end, where " D " Company, 46th Royal Fusiliers, had some house-to-house fighting; but by bold use of their Stokes gun section, which advanced close behind the attacking troops, under Lieutenant W. P. Culbert, and opened fire on the houses, they were soon able to overcome the resistance, and by 1 p.m. the whole village was reported clear, with the capture of about 300 prisoners. A large number of the enemy had fled in disorder across the plain between the village and the Dvina River, the majority of whom escaped to Borok, though a few were shot down by Lewis guns and rifle fire.

At 1.15 p.m. a platoon went to Leushinskaya, which proved to be unoccupied, and was seized without resistance.

At about this time Captain de Miremont, having

mopped up the west end of the village, despatched one platoon, under Lieutenant A. C. Jones, to seize a battery of 4·2-inch guns, which was in action on the edge of the forest. A desperate fight for the guns ensued, Lieutenant Jones making three separate attempts to capture the guns, but being on each occasion met by fire at point-blank range. When this battery was eventually captured later in the day, it was found to have been manned by a crew of German gunners.

Lieutenants Culbert and Jones both received Military Crosses for their work that day.

The troops were organized in a defensive position, with a view to dealing with the large number of the enemy who were known to have been cut off in the Selmenga positions, and who were expected to make an attempt in the course of the afternoon to fight their way back through our lines. At about 3.45 p.m. these troops appeared emerging from the forest in large numbers in extended order, and immediately came under our Lewis gun and rifle fire, one section of the 241st Light Trench Mortar Battery co-operating.

The Bolo line was the most perfect target imaginable. Terrific execution was wrought in their ranks. They advanced just a few yards, and then their spirit was broken. The whole line turned and ran. Reorganizing in the forest, they went round to the north side of the village, where they again came under fire from the posts on that side, and were also taken in enfilade fire from an outlying Lewis gun post. This was too much for the enemy, who were now thoroughly disorganized, the majority of them throwing down their arms and surrendering, while others ran off into the forest, some of whom were afterwards rounded up.

During the night and following morning small groups of the enemy continued to come in from the forest. The total number of prisoners captured by this column was approximately 750, while at least 40 of the enemy were killed (1 Regimental Commander and 2 Battalion Commanders were included among the prisoners).

As the whole attack was an absolute surprise, the booty secured was most pleasing. It included 9 guns, 16 transport carts, 16 machine guns, 5 trench mortars, 900 rifles, 70,000 rounds S.A.A., 500 shells, 200 Stokes shells, 30 telephones, and a large quantity of secret documents, orderly-room papers, etc.

Yet the total casualties to the whole Gorodok column only numbered 12 (3 killed and 9 wounded).

The success of the operation was due primarily to the element of surprise, the attack being carried out at the enemy's meal-hour, and our troops being in the village before the alarm could be given ; to the great dash and spirit shown by all troops, British and Russians alike, who, splendidly led by most enterprising officers, pushed forward without a check to the final objective, sweeping aside all opposition on the way ; and to the splendid co-operation of all arms— artillery, Stokes guns, Lewis guns, and rifles—especially of the Stokes guns.

Pleasure was general at the subsequent news that Major Percival, D.S.O., M.C., had been awarded a bar to his D.S.O. for the day's work. No one deserved it more.

IN RUSSIA.

The Review on Troitsa Heights after the completion of the Attack and immediately before the Withdrawal by General Lord Rawlinson.

IN ENGLAND.

General Lord Rawlinson and the Chaplain–General to the Forces presenting and consecrating the Colours at Sandling, Kent, in May.

A few of the many other awards should be given here.

THE MILITARY CROSS.

Temporary Captain Clive Featherstone, 1st South African General List (formerly 241st Trench Mortar Battery and 46th Royal Fusiliers).

> "He was in command of a light trench mortar battery during the attack on Gorodok on August 10th, 1919. He showed great gallantry and skill under heavy fire in getting his guns close up behind the infantry after the first objective had been taken, and greatly assisted the infantry in the capture of the second objective."

Lieutenant Charles Dawson Moorhead, Manchester Regiment, attached 46th Royal Fusiliers.

> "During the attack on Gorodok on August 10th, 1919, he displayed great gallantry and initiative. During the enemy counter-attack, though wounded, he continued to command his men, and showed great energy and skill in the handling of his platoon."

BAR TO DISTINGUISHED CONDUCT MEDAL.

130560 Sergeant T. G. Goodchild, D.C.M., 46th Royal Fusiliers.

> "During the attack on Gorodok on August 10th, 1919, he displayed great courage and determined leadership. During the enemy counter-attack he held on with seven men and drove the enemy back. He twice attacked a battery of artillery, and finally

I

captured four field guns and twenty-one prisoners, two trench mortar guns, and a large quantity of shells."

THE DISTINGUISHED CONDUCT MEDAL.

180525 Sergeant H. F. Gascoigne-Roy, 46th Royal Fusiliers.

"During the attack on Gorodok on August 10th, 1919, he displayed great gallantry and able leadership under very heavy fire. He captured, with the aid of one section, 85 of the enemy. During the whole attack he did splendid work."

129059 Corporal A. W. Card, 46th Royal Fusiliers.

"He showed conspicuous gallantry during the enemy counter-attack on Gorodok on the afternoon of August 10th, 1919. He rushed his section into position in a remarkably short time under heavy fire, assisted his gun teams in their work, and set a fine example to all troops in the vicinity."

129407 Sergeant G. H. Templeman, 46th Royal Fusiliers.

"During the attack on Gorodok, August 10th, 1919, he displayed great gallantry and initiative in maintaining communication under difficult conditions. During the approach march he succeeded in laying lines throughout, and on reaching the assembly position quickly opened up communication. As the attack proceeded he established forward stations under fire."

123

The only serious opposition on the right bank was that shown to the advance of the Borok column, commanded by Major Nightingale, M.C., of the 46th Royal Fusiliers. The sentries in the Bolo entrenchments were on the alert, and the moment the advance was begun fire was opened upon the oncoming troops. Trouble arose from the machine guns in the left rear, and these had to be dealt with. The first objective was a line outside Borok village itself. In advancing to this line, two officers became casualties, Lieutenant Taylor being killed, and Lieutenant Curtis being wounded in the eye.

The latter's splendid work before that is shown by the *Gazette* notice of the award to him of the Military Cross.

" 2nd-Lieutenant Walter Stopford Constable Curtis, Somerset Light Infantry, attached 46th Royal Fusiliers.

" For gallant and determined leadership. He led his platoon in the attack on Borok on August 10th, 1919. He organized an attack on a strong enemy position on the banks of the Teda River, and outflanked it. He was wounded whilst leading the final assault up the hill, but his platoon captured the position, enabling the remainder of the company to proceed towards the first objective."

The enemy had very well dug trenches and an excellent field of fire, enabling him to hang on for some considerable time. Eventually he was dislodged, and the advance to the second objective, the other side of

I 2

Borok, was commenced. The attack was held up this time, owing to the necessity for lengthening the range of our own guns. Communication with Sector Headquarters was bad at this period, and various delays ensued. Borok was eventually occupied completely shortly after 3 p.m., 102 prisoners taken, 2 field guns, and large quantities of battle transport and stores.

Unfortunately, a most gallant officer, Captain Harry Driver, D.S.O., M.C., of the Bedfordshire Regiment, lost his life, being hit in the stomach by a machine-gun bullet. His death was universally regretted.

     *   *   *   *   *

Thus ended the blow delivered at the Bolshevik forces opposing us. The results were most serious for him. He had lost out of his 6,000 effectives at least 3,700 killed, wounded and missing. Hundreds of Bolos were lost in the woods, and, being without food, must have perished from exhaustion.

In guns and equipment his losses were enormous. We captured 18 guns, 50 machine guns, 2,600 rifles, 7 trench mortars, 12 horses, 17 carts, 60 telephones, and thousands of rounds of gun and rifle ammunition.

In short, he was entirely crushed as an offensive or as a force at all on the Dvina, for those remnants which remained were thoroughly disorganized and cowed.

The success of the operation was due to the loyal and whole-hearted co-operation of all arms of the Army, the sister service, the magnificent fighting qualities of the troops, and the fine and skilful leading by the regimental officers.

The pluck and endurance of the British infantry was

wonderful. The troops were without food for twenty-four hours before the attack, owing to all pack transport having to be abandoned ; but despite this, and though dead tired and soaking wet, the dash and spirit with which they attacked was beyond all praise.

It is interesting to conclude this chapter with the Bolshevik account of the battle. I regret that a brother journalist should be at such variance with myself over so simple a matter as a battle, but I can only say that my account is truthful, while his has some evidences of colouring about it, for I have never yet known British soldiers throw away rum, nor heard of anyone who has.

The article in question was translated from the Bolo paper, *Our War*, the organ of the Political Department of the Northern Army, dated September 5th, 1919.

On August 10th the enemy started an offensive on both banks of the Northern Dvina. As usual, the White Army Mob did not act openly, but did a dirty trick in trying to outflank our troops.

In most cases an outflanking movement is always calculated to have a moral effect. That is rather a nasty thing, as men are nervous and demoralized.

The White Guards thought they had already gained a victory, but they were badly mistaken. The Comrades of Headquarters of N—— Rifle Brigade, situated 1½ versts from the outflanking column of the enemy, saw that it would be bad if the enemy broke through and developed his success. Therefore, at once, everyone belonging to the Political Department of the N——

Region Brigade Headquarters Commandant's troops rapidly armed themselves, under the leadership of the Commander of Headquarters, Comrade Antropov, and counter-attacked the enemy, who was in great strength, at least eight companies, with machine guns, bomb-throwers, and mine-throwers.

At the same moment the comrade sailors of the North Dvina Flotilla opened a deadly artillery fire on the advancing enemy. The White Army, thinking that our brave fellows counter-attacking them formed part of our reserves, hesitated and started a rapid and disorderly retreat ; then our heroes, rapidly forming a cavalry unit, pushed forward and followed the White Man. Seeing this, the White Guard, in a panic and shouting " Cavalry," fled into the wood, throwing away their rifles and ammunition, equipment, and a lot of bottles of rum.

The enemy ran for all he was worth into the woods, where he perished in swamps ; while our heroes, not losing a man, took quite a few villages which previously were held by the Whites. A handful of heroes, with the help of the flotilla artillery, dispersed eight companies of White troops, and prevented them from advancing for three days, until the arrival of reinforcements.

On the same day and time happenings of a similar character took place on the right bank of the river, the enemy trying to outflank our troops here also. He tried a deep out-flanking movement with three columns, about 2,500 men strong, fully equipped, and even with mountain artillery. One of the outflanking columns, protected by the forest, appeared in front of our barbed

*wire and trenches, which were occupied by dismounted
cavalry of N——— Division.*

*The cavalry was carrying out its duties very in-
attentively, and allowed the enemy to surround the
regiment : but this regiment, fighting heroically, broke
through and escaped past the advancing enemy. At this
time still smaller numbers of heroes arrived to our
assistance—namely, the A.S.C. details to N——— Brigade,
at their head their chief, Tabor, and Commissar Klinin.
This handful of heroes threw themselves fearlessly against
the enemy, marched 10 versts, and occupied the village,
where they dug in. The enemy, thinking them to be
our reinforcements, did not dare to continue his advance,
satisfying himself in sending out a squadron of planes
which bombed our heroes with bombs, mines, and gas
bombs.*

*Afterwards the enemy began firing at this village with
heavy artillery. Regardless of this all our supply
heroes held the village. In this way two small parties
gave the Ginger Englishman and the White Guard Filth
a sound thrashing, so that these oversea pigs do not dare
to show their noses up to now. That is what happens
if one does not lose control and gives a good hiding to
rude blackguards.*

*Let them not think that with their low down flanking
movements they can conquer us. No ; great is the power
and might of the soldiers of the Red Army.*

*Comrades of the Red Army, take an example from your
heroes and learn from them !*

*They did splendid work, and proved that, besides the
knowledge of using the pen and supplying troops with*

128

baked bread, in a critical moment, regardless of their lives they can throw themselves into an attack against superior forces of the enemy and make them run away in panic.

With more of this kind of fighter it would not take long to deal with the Filthy White Guard dirt.

Honour and Glory to those heroes of Brigade Headquarters Department of Supplies.

[FROM THE EDITOR.]

Extremely glad for the correspondence of Comrade Gidrassow, who tries to draw the picture as it was.

This kind of correspondence is most important. Only in this way we can learn the reasons of our defeat, and in future take preventive steps.

It is not possible, it seems, to sit in the trenches like moles in a hole and wait till the Englishman comes and in one blow cuts us in two.

Something else is needed.

We know the places where flanking movements are impossible.

Comrades, the organization of communication with the rear of the White Guard warns us against being outflanked.

Be on your guard, and think how to win.

CHAPTER IV

HOW WE CAME HOME TO DEVON.

To leave out from this chronicle the deeds of the other branches of the service during the Dvina battle would be unthinkable. In their particular spheres of activity, their efforts were imbued with the same determination as were the efforts of the infantry. Engineers, signallers, supply corps, all auxiliary services, contributed to the general success only by their grit and pertinacity.

The 885 Field Company, Royal Engineers, under Major Luby, D.S.O., from the date of their arrival at Troitsa, were kept appallingly busy. Roads and *preestens* were made at Troitsa and Yako, and heavy bridges were built at Kurgomin, Savina, Kulgas, and Yako. Civilian working parties were continuously employed by the Engineers. The R.E. encampment on Troitsa beach was by far the most famous spot for the beautiful *barishynas* to foregather. At times there were hundreds of women and girls there, waiting for employment on any type of manual work at 20 roubles a day. And they did work, putting their menfolk to shame.

Owing to the fall of the river, much of the artillery used in the operations in June had been stranded. This was all salved and brought into action. The work was of considerable difficulty, as in some

cases the guns were in very inaccessible places, on
barges in shallow, unnavigable water. Special rafts
had to be built to carry 60-pounders and 155-mm.
howitzers, and the work of getting the guns to the
rafts often necessitated man-handling them with tackle
up slopes and over sandy islands. Several long bridges
had to be built for these guns, and there was considerable difficulty in getting up the material necessary
for the work.

An Ordnance dump was salved in " Jerusalem "
pontoons down a channel so shallow that it would not
permit of any boat drawing more than a foot of water
to pass.

A small barge was salved from up a creek by dam-
ming the creek and pumping water into it with a
Merryweather pump. This barge has been most valuable for carrying stores, etc., in shallow water.

The night of August 9th saw one section in the line
and one in reserve on each bank of the Dvina, with
orders, on the right bank, to repair and make good the
bridge over the Selmenga River, destroyed by the
Bolo in his retreat, and, on the left bank, to make good
the forest track around the Bolo flank.

The forward section on the right bank spent the night
of August 9th-10th in the line, and at midday on
August 10th, after the barrage had lifted, an officer
with a small party of sappers, and covered by an
infantry patrol, proceeded to reconnoitre the bridge.
A sunken road led to the river bank, and the passage
of this was made without mishap ; but on emerging
on to the bank a heavy fire was opened on the party

from the opposite bank of the river, which rendered a close examination of the bridge impossible. The party withdrew, and in doing so one of the covering party was killed.

Repeated attempts throughout the day to reach the bridge were unsuccessful, owing to opposing fire, until about 4.30 in the afternoon, when the bridge was reached and the necessary arrangements made for repairing it.

The section arrived at the site at about 7 p.m., and by 10.30 p.m. the bridge was ready for the passage of transport.

The section bivouacked for the night of August 10th-11th at Selmenga, and in the early morning of August 11th pushed on to the village of Gorodok. Here billets were obtained, and clothes, boots, etc., dried—a much-needed state of affairs. On the morning of August 12th the section moved on again to Oserodok, where billets were obtained, the officers pushing on to Borok and making a reconnaissance of the surrounding forward area. Here roads and tracks were improved, and bridges prepared for demolition.

The right flank column was unable to get the transport out of the forest owing to the marsh, and so No. 2 Section went into action from then as infantry.

Having become separated from the 45th Royal Fusiliers, they entered Kochamika about 3 p.m., and, seeing some men preparing to land from enemy ships in the river, engaged them with Lewis gun fire. A monitor then came down river from the direction of Puchega and drove them out with shell fire. The section then retired to Sludka, and, having avoided a party of between 50 and 60 Bolo Marines, who had landed between Sludka and Zaniskaya, moved into Sludka and found it empty, the 45th Royal Fusiliers having killed or captured all the occupants. The section then pushed on to Lipovets, where it joined the 45th Royal Fusiliers, arriving there at 6 p.m. From then on it moved with the battalion, but had practically ceased to exist as a separate unit, owing to having become separated in the fighting. The various units finally reassembled at the camp near Headquarters, village Yako, by the evening of the 11th.

No. 4 Section and 2nd Labour Company, S.B.L., moved up to Nijni Seltso on the capture of that village at 7 p.m., in order to repair the bridge over the River Sheika if required. It was not possible to get to the bridge until 3 a.m. on the 11th, and it was then found to be in good repair, and fit to carry field guns. The section and S.B.L. remained billeted in Nijni Seltso until the 12th, and then returned to the village of Yakolevskoe.

THE MACHINE GUNNERS.

The 201st Battalion M.G.C. was broken up into groups and attached to the various columns. On the left bank the two sections were in command of Major R. St. G. Mayne, who subsequently took over the Sludka column when Major Shepherd was killed. The progress of the machine gunners was retarded greatly by the heavy marshes. Tripods and guns were carried on Russian ponies till a point was reached when all material had to be man-handled, though it was hoped the ponies would cross later. Only two guns per section were taken from this point, and all extra men were employed in carrying belt-boxes.

For about 4 versts the track led through long strips of very deep marsh, with small patches of forest, a single slippery plank crossing the marsh.

The attack was made on Kochamika and Jitna, and they were soon taken. Four guns pushed on to the river bank, and below them were seen many paddle steamers and barges and two gunboats. The four guns opened fire on their targets, and were engaged by a 6-inch gun in reply.

The attack was moving on Sludka, and the four guns followed. About this time Major Mayne took over command of the column. After Sludka had been taken, and Lipovets, the guns moved on to the latter village.

At the passage, on the 11th, of the Sheika River, as the machine guns were crossing, fairly heavy fire was opened by the Bolos in rear.

The guns crossed and were mounted, and fire was opened. The Bolo fire was soon silenced, and the rest of the column crossed safely. About 50 dead Bolos were afterwards counted at this point, all killed by machine-gun fire. Bolo fire was opened again, but was silenced by the machine guns.

The guns covered the retirement of the infantry from this point, being gradually withdrawn after the wounded had been cleared. Fire was continually opened by the Bolos, but each time it was silenced.

The behaviour of Major Mayne, Lieutenants Harrison

and Armstrong, during these operations was especially
fine. Their energy and initiative in getting the guns
to the assembling point, their coolness under fire, and
their successful efforts in bringing in all their wounded,
are all worthy of the highest praise.

Corporal Kilby showed great coolness in his effort
to help and bring in the wounded ; and Corporal Norton
and Lance-Corporal Parry handled their guns throughout the operations in a very skilful manner.

Lieutenant Fricker was in command of the section
co-operating with the attack on the other bank. The
trek was very difficult in places, and progress was
slow. One gun was posted to form a protective block ;
the other guns remained in reserve, and later were
moved up to take up positions to cover Gorodok.

Several times they were able to open fire on parties
of Bolos. Later the guns moved on to Borok. Though
this section had little firing to do, they showed great
cheerfulness and energy in overcoming the difficulties
of the country.

Other groups of Russian and British guns, under
Captain Webb, Lieutenants Powell and Harvey, performed most useful barrage work. The Russian
companies showed great keenness, and their moral
improved very much after the first few belts. Their
chief difficulties were inability to estimate the rate of
fire, and forgetfulness to oil up and refill.

THE SIGNAL COMPANY.

The plight of the force in action without wireless
would have been pitiable indeed. Fortunately, when

all other means of communication failed, the wireless worked with seemingly renewed vigour, and at no time was there a cessation of communication.

For the month previous to the operation the 250th Signal Company, R.E., was employed on laying a telephone system on strong poled routes, and clearing the area of stray lines. This system was pushed as far forward as possible, and the benefit was reaped during the operations. These lines required but little maintenance, and thereby released more men for work in connection with the forward operations.

The difficulties, almost insurmountable at times, of laying cable can be more readily appreciated after reading the account of the trials of the section on the left bank :—

" The difficulties encountered in maintaining communication during these operations were almost superhuman, owing to the conditions of a country covered with dense forests and intersected by large areas of bog and morass. The only path to the forming up lines was by means of a narrow track. The natural difficulties were intensified by the weather, which was extremely bad, and demanded the greatest physical effort from men and animals.

" The cable used for line communications was D3 and D2, carried on pack animals. Each animal was able to carry two miles of D3 single and half a mile of D2 single. The cable-laying parties went forward with the advanced guard of the infantry, as otherwise the column of infantry and transport, confined to a narrow track, would have interfered with the work, and communication would have been delayed.

" On the first day the cable was laid out by means of a barrow drawn by a pony, but this method was subsequently abandoned owing to the narrowness and roughness of the track, which was often blocked by fallen trees and exposed roots, as well as stretches of bog and deep mud.

" On the second and subsequent days the cable was laid by hand, a stick being used for a spindle. This proved to be a most effective method, as it was possible to make slight detours into the forest to avoid bad places, and it also involved less physical exertion than the attempt to control a heavy barrow bumped over uneven ground of a most poisonous description.

" The pack animals carrying the cable accompanied the cable-laying party, and were always kept about 100 yards in advance.

" The cable-laying party consisted of six men, working in frequent shifts, two men carrying the drum and one man pulling off the cable. A short distance behind this party followed a building party of three men with long crook-sticks, putting the cable high up on to trees out of reach of the traffic and horsemen.

" During the second day the Seltso column branched off, and an exchange was established at the infantry post there, on to which the line back and the two lines forward were led. A party of three infantry signallers was left here.

" On the third day an impassable bog was reached, over which it was found impossible to take either pack animals or heavy drums of cable, especially as this was the first of a series of similar obstacles. The line was therefore continued by D2 cable, the drums being man-handled.

" The previous method of laying out the cable was found satisfactory, but made easier by using the lighter cable.

" At this point it was found equally impossible to get the wireless set farther. The wireless station was therefore erected on the edge of the bog, and a telephone left at the station ' T-ed ' into the cable line forward. By this means communication was maintained the whole time from battle headquarters until the attack was launched, and subsequently until after Sludka was taken.

" Telephonic communication would have been maintained between Force Headquarters and the attacking columns during the whole of the operations but for the fact that units bringing up the rear of the column cut down the trees on which the cable was laid, in order to repair and make good the track across bogs and bad places, making it impossible to keep the lines intact over such considerable distances and with the small personnel available. Touch was lost with the wireless station when the supply of cable ran out, and the party was surprised and cut off by the counter-attack by the Bolo marines.

" The wireless was in touch at every stage in the operations except whilst on the move."

K

The Artillery.

The gunners had most extraordinary obstacles to contend with. Everything seemed to be against them—ground, weather, and observation.

The artillery programme for preliminary bombardment was carried out, with the exception of the chemical bombardment by 18-pounders, which was much curtailed by serious breakdowns. One gun went out of action from a broken valve. This was partially rectified by a wooden substitute, but for the rest of the day this gun could only fire slowly.

Although the artillery bombardments were quite simple, the result reflected great credit on all units concerned.

The Royal Navy had only taken over the 60-pounders a few days previously, and had little or no previous experience of this or any other land gun ; while the Mark IV 18-pounders only arrived from the base on the morning of the 9th, and could not be got into action till 8 p.m. The personnel was found by the Divisional Ammunition Column, none of whom had ever seen this equipment before, assisted by three men who had accompanied the guns from base.

The 2nd S.B.L. Battery had never been in action before, and were required to man five guns with personnel for four ; and the 2nd Russian Battery manned five guns with personnel for four. This battery had been divided into two sections on opposite sides of the river for some months until a few days before the operation.

Much arduous work was cheerfully performed by all ranks in preparation of the operations, and the work of the artillery was, without question, the one potent factor that aided the infantry to gain so decisive a victory.

The chronicle of the work of the guns would be incomplete without a description of the naval 60-pounders. Here it is :—

" On August 1st we landed as a naval detachment to man a 60-pounder field gun. We consisted of three officers, a doctor, and eighteen men taken from the crews of H.M.S. *Humber* and H.M.M. " M. 27."

" The gun provided was a fairly old one, and having some time been immersed in the Dvina River, had not benefited much by the experience. Still, it was a gun, and what else mattered ? We landed at 9.30 a.m. on Luby's Landing, and found our gun being ' assembled ' near the beach. It was ready for removal by 6 p.m., and was taken that night to Yako Church village.

" To move the gun sixteen Russian ponies were supplied, and about thirty Russians, and a most amusing spectacle the removal must have been—much dust, much noise, and the detachment panting in the rear, trying to keep up with the procession.

" On arrival at Yako we were billeted in houses near the gun, and, with the exception of swarms of flies, were really quite comfortable.

" From the 2nd to the 4th of August we were busy building a platform. Luckily, we were given Lieutenant L. A—— as Liaison Officer, and everything was ready by the morning of August 4th. We had our

K 2

first shoot in the afternoon—quite a humorous affair, as in aiming at one machine gun post we accidentally hit another that no one knew anything about.

" From August 4th to 9th we had several minor ' hates '; not that we boasted of having done much execution, but we learnt a good deal in experience, and became accustomed to the idea of aiming at a post behind in order to hit something in front. I am afraid our drill gave the Liaison Officer ' the dry heaves,' but we managed things in our own curious way, and somehow made the piece work.

" On the 7th we shifted the gun and the billets to North Post Wood in readiness for the battle to come. In spite of the flies, we were sorry to say good-bye to our Mrs. Dobra in Yako, and the change to tents was not greatly appreciated, especially as the rain had come.

" On August 9th five more men arrived, and also another gun. This piece had *not* been in the Dvina River, and, what was better still, was completely equipped with every accessory one could imagine. The hoisting of the gun on shore was a critical business, and it was only due to the presence of mind shown by the Russian crane-workers that the gun did not fall on top of the roof of a hospital barge. That it did land safely was certainly not our fault !

" Having got it ashore, the next thing was to get it to North Post Wood. We had many horses and many men, but 5 a.m. on August 10th saw us stuck, with still two miles to go. Luckily, a company of Russians turned up about 6 a.m., and we just managed to get the gun into position in time.

" At 11 a.m. we commenced a furious bombardment of the Bolos, and the next hour was really hard work. We ceased fire at noon, whilst the infantry attacked, and did not open fire again until later on in the day, when, the first attack having failed, the second attack was in progress. Our target from 4.30 p.m., on and off until 7 p.m., was a section of road along which the Bolos were expected to retreat. After 7 p.m. we had no further targets, and we understood that the action had been successful, though certain of the enemy positions had to be cleared up.

" After the Battle of Seltso we remained in North Post for one week more, and we all had a splendid time. No Bolos, but plenty of duck !"

The Royal Army Service Corps.

We have seen how the D.A.D.S. and T. supplied both banks with enormous quantities of transport. But he and his staff did infinitely more. Although the troops were in possession of iron rations for the following day—zero plus one—the D.A.D.S. and T. (Major Watson) pushed rations forward during the night of August 10th-11th, and also sent the Supply Officers up to get in touch with the Officers Commanding Columns.

On the right bank the convoy left at 9 p.m., and Lieutenant Nicholson reported at 4.30 a.m. on the following day that the rations had been safely delivered. He also took up with his convoy twenty carts of small-arms ammunition, which were also handed over.

With the left bank it was extremely hard to keep in touch and to get information as to the exact location of the several columns. It was not until 9.80 a.m. on the 11th inst. that 2nd-Lieutenant Jones reported that all was correct.

If the infantry found the passage difficult, the trials and tribulations of the Supply Officers, with columns of droskies laden with rations, can hardly be imagined.

Strictly speaking, the scope of this work includes only the operations on the Dvina front above Troitsa. Yet I have been led to include in this chapter a short account of the operations entered into by the details of the Sadleir-Jackson Brigade. These details were composed of 150 of the 45th Royal Fusiliers, 100 of the 46th Royal Fusiliers, and 80 of the 201st Battalion M.G.C. They arrived at Archangel on July 12th, expecting to be sent straight to the forward area. The low state of the river prevented this, however. One of the officers of the details has kindly supplied the narrative of events which follows :—

" Four days passed before any more news was forth-coming, and then it was to the effect that some of us might be sent to another front. This news was welcome, as, although all wanted to join their own battalions, it was agreed anywhere was preferable to the Base and its frequent rumours of mutiny and assassination.

" On July 16th O.C. M.G.C. details had orders to embark at Sobornia Quay in charge of his own and the 46th Royal Fusiliers details.

" We were to quell a mutiny, protect ' staffs,' hold an important point on the railway line, and do a hundred other small jobs. We left the quay for

Archangel *preesten*, and, taking train there, proceeded to Oboyerskaya, the Headquarters of the Vologda force, under Brigadier-General Turner, C.M.G., D.S.O.

" Arriving here at about 4 a.m., and acting on previous instructions, we reported to one Staff Captain, to hear the following from the inside of a mosquito curtain :

" ' Oh ! 150 men, 8 M.Gs. Well, I don't know what you are to do. Will you look in about ten o'clock.' And this after we had heard tales which put the Indian Mutiny in the shade !

" However, after a day here something did happen, for on July 19th it was reported that two days later the Bolos proposed to attack, and, aided by friends in the Russian units, carry all before them, and decapitate all British officers.

" On receiving this news, the Staff acted at once, and decided to withdraw the companies in the line, as these were reported to be pro-Bolo. This was done on the 20th, and the companies withdrawn were disarmed by ' Harcourt's Force,' as the details were now called. Many of these men were ultimately shot.

" The Bolo carried out his proposed attack, and captured six block-houses. These six were behind our front system, and consequently the troops there were cut off. At the same time the railway line was blown up in two places to prevent our armoured train from going up to bombard the enemy from close range. Machine gunners were sent out to drive off and keep away this demolition party, which they did until the line was repaired. Immediately that was done fifty

46th Royal Fusiliers and a ' Young Soldiers ' Russian Company went through to counter-attack the Bolo.

" A little earlier than this about a hundred 45th Royal Fusiliers had arrived, and had been sent forward to prevent the enemy from penetrating farther. This they did successfully until relieved by the counter-attacking party. The attack was carried out at dawn, and easily adjusted the situation, capturing a few prisoners and gaining touch with the forward positions.

" This was the first occasion upon which we had worked with Russian artillery, and, not having an interpreter on the spot, the arranging of the barrage was funny in the extreme. Most of it was done by fixing the clock hands at the minute fire was wanted, and then by hand demonstration showing the battery commander that he was to fire like hell. The hand was then moved to zero, and after repeated ' Neito boom !—boom !' we told him that he was to cease fire. Except for the rate of fire, the barrage was a fair success.

" Harcourt's Force then took over part of the line, and were favoured with a heavy attack that night. This was quite safely driven off without any casualties being sustained by the defenders.

" On the 23rd a small patrol which went out to look for signs of the enemy found about 300 of them in a ' slashing ' about one and a half versts from our position. This was passed to the rear with a request that we might be allowed to go out and clear the party off. It was refused, as the ' powers that were ' decided to send a party composed of the 45th Royal

Fusiliers, Australians, and some of the Australian section 201st M.G. Battalion, from behind to drive them off. A little later a prisoner was caught by us who verified the patrol report, but put the enemy at 500 strong.

" The new party, eighty strong, went out about midday, and by working down each side of the slashing where the enemy were drew level with them, and then closed in and by sheer pluck and audacity drove them away in a colossal rout, killing about thirty and bringing a few prisoners back.

" This successful operation ensured a quiet night, as the party were out to drive us right out of our positions and back towards Archangel. With this minor operation, the situation became normal, plus the great advantage that the moral of the Russian troops was well up.

" British patrolling became very active. We went behind his lines almost daily, saw all his working arrangements, counted trains and transport, traced telephone wire, and invariably ' snaffled ' prisoners. These prisoners were all taken without trace, as at this time our 'planes were dropping propaganda in the Bolo areas, telling them how to come over to us and be happy. Later on we found out that the Bolo was unable to account for the disappearance of these men, and took great care that news of a ' desertion ' was not spread among units. It is interesting to note that one prisoner taken carried the only revolver in a certain battery from which a prisoner was much wanted, and was out collecting mushrooms for the day's food.

" Frequent patrols were sent out into the forest on either side of the railway to clear up rumours of enemy raiding parties. These patrols had very strenuous days, as it was nothing to have to penetrate 15 versts and go through wide expanses of heavy bog. Several of the patrols were away forty-eight hours or more, and none less than twenty-four.

" In between times portions of the lines of communication were taken over by the details of either the 45th or 46th Royal Fusiliers, aided by the 201st M.G. Battalion details, and later by " C " Company of that Battalion.

" Several schemes were submitted to Headquarters for raids upon the enemy's lines of communication. These had all been carefully planned and considered, and although approved, it was impossible to carry them out at the time.

" About July 20th rumours of a Russian offensive on the railway were heard, but, strange to relate, we were told that we would not be allowed to help. The way in which the news was received can be left to imagination ; but our spirits went up later, when, after requests to Headquarters, General Lord Rawlinson, during a visit, stated that he had decided to allow us to take a part.

" The rôle we were to play was that of a flanking party. Our objectives were all the enemy's gun positions, and, if possible, at least one armoured train.

" The attack was timed to take place at 5.30 a.m. on July 29th, and on the day previous to this we started to trek through the forest to an assembly position behind the enemy's lines and in towards his guns. At dawn the following morning we were to work close up to them and carry them by storm at 5.15 a.m., fifteen minutes before zero time. As our objectives were widely distributed, two Russian companies from the B.N.R.R. were given to us, one being allotted to the Australian detachment (45th Royal Fusiliers details), under Major May, and one to Major Harcourt's force (46th Royal Fusiliers details and " C " Company 201st M.G. Battalion). While the main forces were taking the large positions, a small party from the Australian detachment was to attack a railway gun on a siding. On zero morning guides led the forces forward, but, unfortunately, took them all to the wrong places. Major Harcourt's force, which should have attacked the large positions from the right front with Major May and the small party to the south of it, found itself at zero minus 20 minutes near the railway siding position, with the other parties still farther south. As it was too late to correct things at this time, Major Harcourt's force decided to attack the siding position and carry that, and then push north to the remaining howitzers, field guns, and mountain guns, relying upon the sound of their attack to bring the other parties up.

" This was started, and after a brisk fight against five machine guns and about eighty men, one 6-inch gun and one ' pom-pom,' five machine guns, and sixty men were captured. This force then reorganized and started to move north for the other positions, when Major May's force came up and went on their right.

The main positions were very soon being attacked, and were carried after a very short fight.

" The mountain guns were taken a few minutes after this by Harcourt's force. The haul at this time was eight guns, five in working order, eight machine guns, and about 180 men. About thirty enemy were killed or wounded. Our casualties were three killed and eight wounded, including Major May.

" The party which was to have taken the gun siding position found itself some distance to the south of these happenings, and in between the two attacks above encountered an armoured train, which they succeeded in driving off, inflicting heavy casualties, and suffering none.

" As orders before the attack warned us to be ready to advance on Emtsa, a village about 6 versts forward, the whole party, less two platoons who garrisoned the captured positions, were collected, and waited ready for orders to advance. These never came, however, as the Russians took longer than they expected to be clear of their objectives, and when they did come forward to us decided to attack Emtsa themselves. The time we were compelled to waste here lost Emtsa for us on that day.

" After this our rôle as attacking troops ceased. We held the position we had taken until September 9th, when we started to move back to the base for embarkation."

As a result of the complete demoralization of the Bolo, life became fairly pleasant in the captured villages once we had settled down. Two or three days were expended in cleaning up the captured area, and the transporting to the forward area of blankets and clothing and stores, badly needed by everyone. To be able to get a change of clothing and to have a rea blanket to sleep in was akin to being billeted in Brussels direct from Ypres.

The villagers viewed us with mingled surprise and pleasure. Naturally, upon our first arrival they welcomed us with exceeding glee. Had we not beaten the Bolsheviks ? Had we not large supplies of food to exchange for their ridiculously scraggy chickens ? But their joy faded a little when authority was exercised. Firstly, the *storastas* were assembled and warned that villagers were suspected of hiding Bolsheviks. Vigorous denials and head-shakings followed the allegation. But the following morning produced many camouflaged soldiery, who found their way with much ease to the various headquarters, and after interrogation were sent to join their incarcerated companions. The rounding up of the rifles and ammunition was not such an easy matter, and dealing with the captured Bolo horses was even more difficult. Every peasant, not unnaturally with an eye to the future, carefully secreted a rifle or two and ammunition. Such weapons were always handy things to have about the house, particularly in days of incessant strife. Very reluctantly the warnings of the *storastas* to deliver up these weapons were obeyed, and the pile for destruction grew higher. But with the horses the question became abstruse in the extreme.

Peasants sauntered round the horse lines with an

apparently indifferent air. In reality they were viewing the animals with a view to claiming them as lost property. One, more bold than the rest, suggested to a transport officer that a mistake had been made. In rounding up the animals he had under his charge, his men, quite by accident, had included the rightful property of the aforesaid peasant. It was not for him to suggest that it was intentional, but under the circumstances—the state of his crops, his large family and their great needs—might his horse be returned by the all-powerful and just English officer ?

Though thoroughly versed in Russian cunning, the transport officer, suspecting nothing, accepted the plausible story, and the peasant rode away in glee on an animal that had probably never been owned either by him or any of his widespread relations. An hour later the transport officer realized his blunder. Fifty Russian peasants regretted that his men had rounded up their horses. It was not for them to suggest—— etc., but the crops——etc. ! ! !

There was one way only out of the maze of inquiries and pleadings. It was to recall the original peasant who had succeeded in his story. His copious tears on having to yield up his newly acquired horse were a tremendous satisfaction to his fifty compatriots, who had failed in their strenuous efforts. Taken generally, however, the peasantry in the captured villages were distinctively friendly. I think it was chiefly inspired by visions of gifts of flour, tea, and sugar, but it was nevertheless welcome after the Bolshevik displays by peasantry in some of the villages behind the

line. Such gifts—and they were manifold—were wise
policy, however. We had before us an evacuation,
and the villagers might have been troublesome. Moreover, it left behind us a good impression.

The Bolshevik forces had apparently disappeared
altogether, save for a few of the stalwart heroes of the
Brigade Headquarters of the Department of Supplies.
On both banks the advance had been pushed a little
farther—on the left to beyond Puchega, and on the
right to beyond Ivanovskaya. The Russian cavalry
came up and helped to establish the forward positions,
giving complete security for the process of evacuation of stores, which was being commenced in the rear.
The base at Bereznik had been almost cleared by this
time of its stores, and the barges and war craft should
have been congregated at Troitsa. Despite the
appalling rain that had fallen, however, the river had
only risen a few inches, and the same difficulties of
navigation were being met with. The work of loading,
nevertheless, proceeded slowly, while the troops in
the line looked forward to the day when the first move
backwards was put into operation.

Psychologically, our attitude had changed as a
result of the big fight. We had performed our relief.
We had given the Bolo a nasty jar, and now we wanted
to get home as soon as possible. Everyone was very
much in the dark about evacuation, though the arrival
of General Lord Rawlinson to co-ordinate the withdrawal had produced a feeling of optimism.

Speculation was rife as to the day we should shake
the sands of Troitsa from our feet. But many stranger

things were to transpire before then, of which we had
no inkling. The first was the formation of the mounted
infantry. Company Commanders asked for volunteers
who could ride horses. The number was legion.
Some rode, some bobbed up and down in the saddles,
some merely fell off, while the remainder showed a
strange hesitancy about mounting.

One of the volunteers from " C " Company, 45th
Royal Fusiliers, was brought in front of the Company
Commander, who questioned him as to his previous
experience ; but no information was forthcoming
except that on one occasion he had acted as the
Colonel's groom for a week.

The officer, thinking he would test the soldier on
technical grounds, asked him if he had ever heard of
thrush.

The soldier's face assumed an expression of blank
amazement, and with a rich Irish brogue he replied :
" Do you mean a bird, sir ?"

He was not sent to the mounted infantry branch.

A review of the troops engaged in the fighting was
held on Troitsa heights by General Lord Rawlinson,
and the flags that had so bravely fluttered to the soft
breezes of Kent, were unfurled on parade. The Naval
detachment made a brave show that review day.

After the attack of August 10th Seltso became quite
a habitable hamlet, and " C " Company, 45th Royal
Fusiliers, became the occupants. However, the quiet
aspect of the village was somewhat disturbed one day
early in September by the sudden influx of able-
bodied civilians.

The officers of the company immediately met in conference to decide who the suspected civilians were.

Several contentions were put forward, the most prominent being that the suspects were Bolo agents who had filtered through our line and were endeavouring to recruit sympathizers. Suspicions rose very high when about sixty young men were discovered in an empty house, and immediately a strong guard with fixed bayonets and bombs was placed around the house.

Similar happenings were reported from other villages, and amazement ran high. The explanation was simple, yet at the same time fraught with seriousness. The Russian authorities had returned all the mobilized men from Puchega and villages farther East. Subsequently, without doubt, many of these were responsible for giving to the enemy up-to-date and first-hand information of the disposition of the British forces. At the time, however, they were an annoyance.

So the month of August dragged, or seemed to drag, along. Towards the end of it the Navy grew busy.

Thirty mechanical mines and thirty large horned mines were laid in the Dvina between August 28th and September 2nd. On September 9th ten mechanical mines and twenty horned mines were laid in the Vaga River.

It is of interest to note that the enemy had not swept the advanced lines of mines until September 19th, over a week after our evacuating Troitsa, and it appears unlikely that his ships got through the main minefields before the ice had set in.

L

With the mining of the river, the rise of water, brought about by the August rains, stopped, and it was obvious the psychological moment had come to get as many ships of the flotilla down as possible. By August 30th all the ships had passed down except H.M. M.25, M.27, and the yacht *Kathleen*, which were of too deep draught.

This had called for exceptional efforts, as it entailed removing heavy guns, mountings, ammunition, and stores, and in some cases even the main engines, to lighten the ships sufficiently.

The Intelligence branch now began to supply us with interesting news—namely, that the Bolshevik had brought up considerable reinforcements, including the Finnish Red Guards—and was proposing to drive " the ginger Englishmen " clean into the sea. This alarmed none.

But on the afternoon of September 6th, about four o'clock, two Bolo battalions began an advance against the outposts on both banks. A strong attack, supported by considerable artillery fire from his flotilla, was opened against the piquet line on the eastern outskirts of Puchega.

The conformation of the ground, and the ease with which the outposts could be outflanked from the south, caused them to fall back fighting across the Kodema River. In this action two other ranks were wounded, and two other ranks were apparently cut off and captured.

The receipt of this grave news resulted in two naval 12-pounders being moved from Yakolevskoe to

Chudinova, and an 18-pounder was also sent up. There were no teams available, so drosky ponies were used instead. The harness was borrowed from the 45th Royal Fusiliers, deficiencies being made good with odd bits of string, etc.

None of the ponies had worked in a team before, and as the normal method employed by the Russian pony to extricate a load stuck fast in the mud is first to retreat as fast as the harness will allow, and then to plunge forward, the state of chaos when a team of eight employs these tactics on a pitch dark night can be left to the imagination.

Each peasant tried to give his own horse as little work as possible, but by arming each man with a stick to beat the pony in front, this difficulty was partly overcome.

Some idea of the roads can be gathered from the following data. Seltso to Lipovets is about three miles; the time taken with a team of eight (and four spare) and a platoon of " D " Company was exactly six hours ; nearly half the distance was accomplished by man-handling.

At every short halt the Russian drivers would set up cries of " Sleepem " and " Scoffem," and when the Bolo on our arrival greeted us with a few shells, the harness was simply flung down, and our transport vanished before anyone realized what had happened.

On the morning of the 7th large parties of the enemy advanced and occupied Kodema, but they suffered somewhat when our guns shelled the village and we destroyed the bridge over the river. Security for the

L 2

subsequent retreat on Seltso, in the process of evacuation, was gained on this bank, and for a while events quietened down.

On the left bank there had been similar demonstrations on the part of the Bolos. About six o'clock on the 6th the enemy, 40 strong, were observed drifting into Ivanovskaya. A party of 20 Mounted Fusiliers and 1 platoon were organized to attack the enemy at dawn. The hostile attack was feeble, and effected nothing. At 2.30 p.m., September 7th, the counter-attack was delivered against Ivanovskaya.

The enemy made fair resistance at first, but was eventually driven out and pursued into the woods. Forty-five prisoners were captured, and 17 enemy corpses were counted. Prisoners stated the wounded exceeded 40. Two more battalions were reported at Nijni Toima.

In this wise began our evacuation troubles.

The Bolsheviks who had had the temerity to enter Kodema experienced a rude awakening the next morning. Two platoons under Captain Fowkes, of the 45th Fusiliers, crossed the river during the night of the 7th, and at three o'clock in the morning delivered a bayonet assault on the enemy holding the village.

Seventeen of them were killed, and the remainder of the " gallant heroes " fled at their utmost speed to Puchega, and the British troops returned after this hour's good work. A mounted patrol spotted at the same time a column of the enemy about 300 strong moving in a north-westerly direction, and subsequently plans were made to attack it.

At 12.80 a bayonet attack was made, followed by
a pursuit by one platoon and a troop of mounted Fusiliers. The bayonet attack was completely successful,
81 of the enemy being killed, and 99 prisoners captured,
in addition to 3 machine guns on wheels.

Quantities of rifles, equipment, and ammunition were
captured and destroyed. The British casualties during
these operations amounted to one other rank wounded.

On the other bank the enemy was even more active
on this day. Five hundred of the Red Guards attacked
the outposts at Ivanovskaya, but the men of the 46th
Royal Fusiliers repulsed them, killing 30, including
10 officers, and numerous wounded. They retired and
attempted to dig in, with considerable interruptions
owing to artillery fire brought to bear on them from
Chudinova.

These attacks by the enemy on the 6th, 7th, and
8th had hardly been profitable to him. The ground
he had gained was a mere fraction, and as we had
intended to give it up in any case, his occupation of
it could hardly be termed a gain. His casualties had
been 168 killed, 200 wounded, 2 officers and 146 other
ranks prisoners. The British casualties were 1 other
ranks killed and 10 other ranks wounded.

Before and during these exciting days the Navy
had been busy evacuating the vessels of the flotilla.
The sand-bars across the Dvina proved considerable
obstructions, and strenuous efforts were made to clear
them. Dredging and the explosion of a large number
of depth charges were resorted to with some success.

for H.M. M.25 was got over two bars, and H.M. M.27 across another. Then the river began to fall again.

H.M.S. *Humber* managed to get down after an event almost unprecedented in the annals of the naval service.

Science has not developed sufficiently as yet to solve the problem of how to steam a ship drawing 6 ft. of water or more through water which is only 5 ft. or less deep.

The sailor men in the *Humber* had to get their ship away; but how? Eventually the order was given: "Lighten ship." Everything that was not essential was taken out of the vessel. Her draught was still too great.

In the *Humber*, however, there was scope for some ingenuity and resource. This particular ship was armoured, having on each side a belt of 3-in. armour running fore and aft, and projecting 2½ ft. below the water-line. It was estimated to weigh 70 tons.

Seventy tons of dead weight was no mean item under the circumstances, and it was decided that this should be removed. Easier said than done. It may be well to observe that those who build ships with armoured sides are in the habit of securing the plates by means of large screw bolts passing through the ship's side and screwed into the armour-plates, and they are fixed so securely in order that they may not be removed till the day when the ship falls to pieces from old age or under the strokes of the shipbreaker.

In the *Humber* each armour-plate weighed about three tons and was secured by six bolts. In order to

get at the boltheads it was compulsory to get into the
wing compartments, which were divided into spaces
3 ft. by 3 ft. by 1½ ft., just enough room for a small
man to get into, but not big enough for him to work in.

The men on board were inspected, and the smallest
men were mustered. Special large spanners had to
be made, and with these and huge hammers the staff
of armour-plate removers began their work.

It took forty-eight hours to get the first plate off,
and it fell into the Dvina River with a mighty splash.
After a few days at this new and diverting game the
men managed to get two and even three plates off
each day, and finally, after a fortnight, the whole of
the plate was lying at the bottom of the river.

The *Humber* then proceeded merrily down stream.

The day before the force actually left the Troitsa
line was a most exciting one. The night of the 8th-9th
passed very quietly; but at seven o'clock on the 9th
the Bolo flotilla opened a heavy bombardment on
Ivanovskaya, and at eight o'clock two battalions of
the Finnish Red Guards delivered a most determined
assault from the north, south, and west of the village.

Ivanovskaya was only held by a small detachment
of mounted men of the 46th Royal Fusiliers, under
Lieutenant Luke Green, M.C. A desperate fight
ensued. Our men came to hand fighting with the
enemy, and Lieutenant Green distinguished himself in
a titanic battle with three Bolos. They suffered,
though Green's small party (" Green's Horse," as we
called them) were by this time completely cut off from
Borok, which Captain de Miremont's company was

holding ; they succeeded in fighting their way back, with the loss of two killed and eight wounded and missing. A D.S.O. was subsequently awarded Lieutenant Green for his cool and skilful withdrawal from this dangerous position.

The Bolo at the same time attacked Borok, but here our forces were in considerable strength, and he was successfully repulsed. Obviously the enemy had good and able leaders, for the tactics and determination shown were distinctly good.

Similar hostile movements were reported from the left bank of the Dvina.

At 10 a.m. a seaplane reported 300 fresh enemy troops arriving at Puchega. At 11.30 a.m. Kodema, Sludka, and Chudinova were heavily shelled by the enemy's flotilla and land batteries. Casualties amongst civilians were inflicted in Sludka. At 2.30 p.m. the enemy recommenced a heavy bombardment on the Kodema defences, but no infantry attack materialized.

An 18-pounder was brought into action from Lipovets against the enemy holding the eastern banks of the Teda River, and the shelling was accurate and effective.

Later in the day events quietened down, but at G.H.Q. matters were moving. General Sadleir-Jackson and Captain Altham, reviewing the situation, considered it tactically unsound to hold on to the Troitsa line under the circumstances. It was proposed to extend the date of evacuation from Troitsa to the 15th instant by G.H.Q. at Archangel. Attempts were still being made to get H.M. Monitors 27 and 25 off sandbars, and, having in mind the tired state of the troops, who had been fighting hard for three days, and the necessity for considerable detachments, the two officers decided to fall back during the night of the 10th, embark at Troitsa and Yakolevskoe, and move down river to a new line in front of Shushega on the left bank and Pless on the right. Orders to this effect were therefore issued.

All through the night the embarkation went on. Barges had previously been loaded with baggage, and the auxiliary units proceeded down river early in the day.

A few of the villagers gathered to see us finally depart. All bridges and pontoons had been blown up as the infantry withdrew from the forward positions, and it was early morning when the last of the men embarked. Perhaps the last act in leaving Troitsa was the firing of the *preesten*. The beach had been denuded, and anything left behind was set alight.

The *preesten* was soaked in oil and set ablaze, and as the last of the convoy left the area, where we had succeeded in so great a victory, the flames leapt high into the air. It seemed a great tragedy to leave the ground we had fought for to the enemy, but it was imperative. All we left behind of material value was the white cross on Troitsa heights that marked the resting place of our dead comrades.

Shushega and Pless were uninteresting places, though it was essential to hold the line here till September 17th. Small parties marched from Troitsa to the new line, leaving well in advance of the river convoy, collecting all available transport from the villages *en route*. Such action was necessary because of the final evacuation from the new line, and further to obstruct the Bolo if he advanced. He did advance, and during the course of the stay at Pless and Shushega he gained contact with our advanced patrols. Even here he suffered, several of his scouts being killed. He attempted no serious attack, however.

Valiant efforts were still being made to float H.M. Monitors 25 and 27, but they were unsuccessful, and finally, after removing everything of value and leaving but the bare shells, the two ships that had served us so well were blown up in a most thorough fashion.

Finally, on September 17th, the convoy recommenced the journey down river, releasing, to their great joy, all the *droskies* we had commandeered, who promptly proceeded to their homes, probably to be remobilized by the advancing Bolos.

The Russians, who were holding a line in rear, actually sent an urgent message begging us to hold the line (Pless—Shushega) as the last of our troops were embarking, although they had had ample time and warning to take over the line.

" C " Company of the 45th Royal Fusiliers was left behind at Shushega to protect the left bank, and as all means of withdrawal had been previously destroyed, it was arranged that the company should be conveyed by small boats to an island in the River Dvina, from where they were to be picked up by fast-moving tugs and rejoin the battalion on the barge.

About 5 a.m. on the morning of the evacuation the O.C. " C " Company decided to test the scheme for the evacuation in small rowing boats, by taking a couple of N.C.Os. in a boat procured from the *Starosta*. The outward journey was accomplished in good time, and after a look round the island the return journey was commenced ; but the difficulties began. After being stuck in mid-stream for two hours and having struck innumerable sandbanks, the party in disgust decided to abandon the boat and walk home, which they did under the eyes of the whole of " C " Company. Everyone seemed to enjoy the position except the O.C. " C " Company and his two partners, who were soaked in icy cold water up to the waist.

At 10 a.m. the evacuation was to be complete, and at 9 a.m. the O.C. " C " Company was informed by the Brigade Major that a tug was coming along to pick up the Company. At 9.30 a.m. the tug duly arrived, dragging behind it six rowing boats, and the evacuation began at once, the *barishynas* rowing the troops from the shore to the tug.

At 10.15 a.m. the evacuation was completed, three bridges being blown sky-high simultaneously with the withdrawal.

The Company Commander, along with his standard-bearer, were the last of the 45th Royal Fusiliers to leave the left bank of the Dvina.

Trouble awaited the convoy at Bereznik, the confluence of the Vaga and the Dvina. The British force holding on the Vaga had handed over to the Russians, but an attack by the Bolo succeeded, and they were able to advance to the mouth of the river.

As the last vessels came down river, machine-gun fire was opened upon them from the left bank of the Dvina. Fortunately, we had a gun barge, under Captain Milton, R.A., and the two 18-pounder guns got to work. General Sadleir-Jackson had a narrow escape when he came down to investigate in a coastal motor boat, for a bullet passed two inches above his head and through the glass screen of the tiny craft.

An armed naval launch and coastal motor boats were also dispatched to counter this, and a Royal Marine detachment under Lieut. Sergeant, R.M.L.I., landed and dispersed the enemy machine gunners, killing three of them.

The casualties in this attack, the final attack by the Bolo, were eleven, the men being hit on one of the barges which the enemy fired upon.

The remainder of the passage down river was uneventful, save for a delay due to grounding of several barges in the shallow and intricate channel off Khoboritza.

The A.S.C. ration barge, with Major Watson and his staff on board, had a thrilling time at this bar, in company with the barge containing the 46th Royal Fusiliers. The latter were lucky, however, for after being hung up for two days all the infantry were removed on tugs and lighters, and the barge abandoned. Not so the ration barge. That remained with the staff. In fact, according to one of the officers on board, the whole voyage down river after Troitsa was a chapter of accidents.

"When the barge (*N.T.* 252) started on the first morning of the evacuation there was a gale of wind blowing, and no sooner had the tug commenced to tow than the barge took charge of the tug. Another tug, to evade being crushed against the *preesten*, manœuvred into position between *N.T.* 252 and its tug, and succeeded in getting the tow-rope round its propeller shaft. After crashing into the hospital barge, the *N.T.* 252 gracefully finished up by bumping the ammunition barge, amidst loud curses from naval officers and Russian skippers.

"After about a couple of hours' hard work, the rope round the shaft was disentangled, and we continued on our way, only to perform similar evolutions on two further occasions. The first of these resulted in the tug being pulled some quarter of a mile out of its course, finally going to ground on a sandbank, but not so badly that it could not pull itself off. The next time we merely proceeded broadside on down-stream, collecting all the navigating lights as we went, and once again trying conclusions with an ammunition barge, until finally we came to rest at our right anchorage. The next few days were really quite uneventful, chiefly owing to the fact that we did not move. Then, on September 15th, we started again, and everything went well for a couple of days.

"September 17th was a glorious day, and in the afternoon the whole barge company was basking in the sunshine, when all of a sudden there was a bump and a jolt, and we discovered that both our tugs and ourselves were hard and fast on a sandbank. The Russian pilots had taken the wrong channel, it appeared. To make matters worse, the Russian bargee, seeing that we were going aground, dropped the anchor before the weigh was off, with the result that the barge sat on the anchor, and a foot of it, including the barb, went through the side of the boat.

" The usual S.O.S. was sent out, but nothing happened, all and sundry being fully occupied in getting themselves off similar sandbanks. Water was coming in rapidly, so a coffer dam was constructed and filled up with lard. This had the effect of making it fairly watertight, and with the continuous use of hand-pumps the water was kept down. Nothing further happened for two days, when an effort was made with two paddlers to pull us off the sandbank. Although they succeeded in moving the barge, we did not get clear of the bank.

" By about midday on September 19th the whole of the other craft had disappeared, and we were left alone on the bar. At about 8 p.m. on this day we were hailed out of the night from a tug, and were informed that a paddler would come to take us off in the early hours of the following morning. About 11 a.m. we saw a tug appearing, but unfortunately it was only able to get to about 200 yards from us. The Naval Transport Officer hailed us, and informed us that the paddler would be up at any moment. Some two hours later the paddler appeared, steaming slowly up stream, but on reaching the lower end of the bar something obviously went wrong ; she turned completely round and grounded on the bar. It afterwards transpired that she had dropped her rudder. The Naval Transport Officer now went back in his tug and towed her into deep water about one mile away from us on the opposite bank across the island. The Naval Transport Officer then came back with his tug and a couple of rowing boats, and we started transferring our kit by means of rowing boats to the Naval Transport Officer's tug, lying in deep water. He, in his turn, conveyed the stores to the paddler. Unfortunately, it was blowing a gale, and the rain was descending in torrents. Apparently this dismayed the occupants of the rowing boats, for after the first journey they disappeared altogether. The wind had also blown the Naval Transport Officer's tug on to the bar, so communication was at an end.

" The morning of September 20th dawned. The barge was still fast aground, and the gale and rain continued. Not a sign of life was visible on the river or on the banks, till at dusk we attracted the attention of a small boy in a rowing boat by firing near him with a rifle. The wretched boy was lighting the lamps on the navigation buoys. He was ordered to produce all available boats from the surrounding villages at dawn the following morning. Dawn arrived, with an increase in the velocity of the wind and the intensity of the rain. There was no sign of a boat anywhere. About eight o'clock the weather cleared, however, and four small rowing boats arrived. The transference of personal kit commenced in dead earnest.

168

" This was a tedious business, as the boats could
only take a small load, and the journey comprised,
first a row across the river to the island, then the stores
had to be man-handled across the island, and thence
again by row boats across another stretch of the river
to where the paddler was lying. However, all was
completed by about 12.20 p.m. Even now we were
without any means of getting on, as although we could
make steam, we required the assistance of another tug
to keep us on our course. The Naval Transport Officer's
tug was still hard aground, so we waited. Presently
a tug was sighted going up stream, and on being hailed
replied that in about an hour it would have finished
the job it was on, and would tow us down to Siskoe.
Having had previous experience of the Russian idea
of time, a boarding party was sent on board, with
instructions to bring the tug back at once. The tug
returned well within the hour, and down stream we
proceeded. After having gone about ten versts, we
came across another tug, and as this was, so its captain
informed us, proceeding to Archangel, and was, moreover, a stronger tug, we dispensed with our present tug
and took this new one.

" All went well for a couple of hours or so, when
suddenly the tug's main steam-pipe burst. There were
no casualties. We were now in the position of having
one paddler that would steam but would not steer,
and one tug that would steer but would not steam.
We accordingly hitched the two together and proceeded on.

" We arrived at Ust Pinega at about 1.30 a.m. on

September 23rd, only to find that the Russian Naval Transport Officer had received instructions to place the skipper of our tug under arrest for absence from duty somewhere up-river. After much argument we managed to convince him that he must proceed to Archangel for repairs to the steam pipe, so at about 6 a.m. we were allowed to proceed, and an additional tug, containing some eighty Bolo prisoners, was also tacked on. Our procession now consisted of three tugs in line. At about 10 a.m. we met two coastal motor boats that had come up river to look for us. Shortly afterwards a monitor and a seaplane also signalled us. Without further mishap we made Headquarters at about 3 p.m. on September 23rd."

The R.A.S.C. barge and personnel therefore was for four days the complete rear guard to the whole force, which shows that it is not only in the Bolshevik army, but in our own, that the department of supplies can be heroes. I should like to have Comrade Gidrassow describe this stirring event, particularly as he would have undoubtedly laid stress on the following incident that happened while the *N.T.* 252 was aground.

All supplies had been handed over to the Russians, less a small amount of rum, which the D.A.D.S. and T. had been instructed to destroy, if unable to carry away. In pursuance of his instructions, Major Watson was busy breaking the bottles over the side of the barge. Hearing yells from below, he glanced over, to behold two natives in a small boat, catching the contents of the bottles in their mouths. The fact of glass descending with the spirit failed to deter them.

M

A short stay was made by the convoy at Lyavlya, where a line was held till September 27th. We were supported there by H.M. Monitors 31 and 33, who had re-armed at Archangel, until the final evacuation.

H.M. Monitor 26 was stationed off Bakharitsa, and H.M.S. *Fox* off Archangel.

The final evacuation on September 27th was conducted in perfect order, the monitors falling back on H.M.S. *Fox* after all river transports had cleared, and preceding that cruiser out of harbour.

The majority of the Brigade travelled home on the ss. *Kildonan Castle*. The trip was wonderful, and we dropped anchor at Plymouth, from whence all ranks were demobilized.

Of all the many congratulatory messages, the only one I shall quote is that of His Majesty King George V. to the Force :—

" *To General Lord Henry Rawlinson.*

" On completion of the evacuation of the Allied troops from North Russia, I desire to congratulate you and all ranks under your command on the successful manner in which this difficult operation has been accomplished.

" I wish to express my appreciation of the skill displayed by the commanders, and the courage, discipline, and power of endurance of all ranks. These qualities have enabled the forces both at Archangel and Murmansk to be withdrawn from their advanced positions in contact with the enemy, transported over great distances to their bases, and embarked with practically no loss of life.

" It is especially gratifying to me to note that the withdrawal has been carried out, in such a manner as to leave the loyal Russian forces in a favourable position for continuing an active and resolute defence.

" GEORGE, R.I."

So ends this short chronicle of our efforts in North Russia. Since we left that country the Bolo has overrun the land and captured Archangel. With the political aspect of the situation we are not concerned. Suffice it to say that certain things were asked of us, and those things we performed.

The officers and men of the Relief Force and the flotilla have parted and gone their various ways into all parts of the world to their homes and their work. That was inevitable. In the words of Candide, the greatest of all philosophers, " *Il faut cultiver notre jardin.*"

But the memories of the days and the nights of Troitsa, and of the loyal comradeship of the Dvina, will never fade.

THE END.

THE GLORIOUS DEAD.

"There's some corner of a foreign field
That is for ever England . . . ."

ROLL OF HONOUR

1st July, 1919, to 30th September, 1919.

" They shall not grow old
  As we that are left grow old.
  Age shall not weary them
  Nor the years condemn
  At the going down of the sun
  And in the morning
  We will remember them."

THE NAVY.

OFFICERS.

Lieutenant R. H. Fitzherbert-Brockholes, R.N.
Mr. Trevor Livesay, Gunner (T.), R.N.
Lieutenant J. Gondré, R.A.F.
Lieutenant Cyril E. McLaughlin, R.N.
2nd-Lieutenant Claude M. Lemoine, R.A.F.
Surgeon-Lieutenant Rowland Thursfield, R.N.
Lieutenant Thomas L. MacFarlane, R.N.V.R.
Captain Dugald MacDougall, R.A.F.
Commander Sebald W. B. Green, R.N.

MEN.

	OFF. NO.
Leading Seaman John Sexton	J.24832
Able Seaman Thomas M. Cheeseborough ...	J.85493
Aircraftsman 1st Class Henry W. Scudder ...	227344
Engine Room Artificer William W. Dennison	279982
Mechanician Charles F. Warren	
Able Seaman James Webb	J.19636
Able Seaman John W. Buss	J.2144
Stoker 1st Class Walter Alexander	311118
Stoker 1st Class Alfred H. Eels	
Officers' Steward 2nd Class Charles W. Nelson	L.4055
Able Seaman Stanley Chisman	
Able Seaman John R. McCoy	S.S.7701
Able Seaman Leonard Glanville	J.90427
Able Seaman Sidney Hill	S.S.8798
Leading Seaman Alexander Keith	195605
Stoker 1st Class John McCrae	K.22922
Armourer's Crew Harold Sykes	J.55280
Able Seaman Edward H. Coate	J.16309
Able Seaman Henry Wright	J.25828
Able Seaman Lancelot W. H. Smith	J.14515
Officer's Steward 2nd Class Joseph Ayres ...	L.625
Signalman Thomas W. Farmer ...	J.33401
Leading Seaman George Dawes ...	J.12484
Leading Seaman Robert G. Cleveland	J.16266

Yeoman of Signals Patrick Casey	...	...	227466
Able Seaman William G. Leadbetter	...	...	J.20444
Able Seaman Ernest Snellgrove		...	J.43244
Able Seaman Frederick Murray	...	...	J.44493

THE ARMY.

OFFICERS.

45TH BN. ROYAL FUSILIERS.

Major S. le F. Shepherd.
Captain G. C. de Mattos.
Lieutenant J. C. Zigolmala, O.B.E.
Lieutenant A. V. Colledge.
Lieutenant Lord Settrington.
Lieutenant A. C. Pearse, M.C.

46TH BN. ROYAL FUSILIERS.

Captain H. Driver, D.S.O., M.C.
Lieutenant G. Jacob, D.C.M., M.M.
Lieutenant W. N. C. Taylor.

R.A.M.C.

Lieutenant G. H. Middleton.

OTHER RANKS.

45TH BN. ROYAL FUSILIERS.

128930	R.S.M.	G. T. Garnham, M.M.
128947	Cpl.	S. Hill.
130934	Pte.	W. Hinson.
129220	,,	E. Gallagher.
130256	,,	G. Robinson.
130269	,,	P. Gledhill.
130253	,,	F. E. Jones.
131583	,,	E. Kelly.
131035	,,	C. Cruise.
129126	,,	W. S. Broadbent.
129617	,,	C. Martin.

180806	Pte.	C. Barry.
180143	,,	T. McLachlan.
130197	,,	W. Cree.
181122	,,	R. Power.
181555	,,	R. Slade.
180961	,,	C. Wren.
181015	L./Cpl.	F. Salisbury.
129796	Pte.	J. Bell.
128952	Sgt.	J. Bettany.
129176	Pte.	J. Fulbrook.
129594	,,	R. Logan.
181476	,,	J. S. Trotter.
130807	L./Cpl.	J. Lawton.
128979	,,	L. G. Robertson.
181207	Pte.	W. E. Wright.
129217	,,	J. O'Neill.
181599	,,	A. Hare.
128970	Sgt.	P. E. Petter, D.C.M.
128960	Cpl.	E. R. Nash, M.M.
181228	Pte.	G. Scott.

46TH BN. ROYAL FUSILIERS.

129880	Sgt.	E. Jackson.
181804	Pte.	W. Brown.
129843	,,	B. Richardson.
180866	,,	E. Pearman.
129315	,,	T. Andrews.
180870	,,	J. Aggle.
180320	,,	W. Gallon.
129303	,,	J. Sliney.
129587	,,	F. Sexton.
129840	,,	J. Wallace.
129213	,,	J. Mahoney.
180850	,,	A. Burrows.
133378	,,	J. Cairns.
133354	,,	J. Stoddart.
133306	Cpl.	J. Mulhall.
129393	Pte.	A. Doyle.

ROYAL ARTILLERY.

Gunner Gracie.   Gunner Bridcutt.

WOUNDED

THE NAVY.

OFFICERS.

Mr. Thomas J. Vosper, Chief Bos'n, R.N.
Lieutenant J. S. Prouse, R.A.F.
Lieutenant Rankin, R.A.F.
Lieutenant-Commander Arthur J. L. Murray, R.N.
Lieutenant Anthony H. G. Thorold, R.N.
Gunner Albert M. Wildbore.
2nd-Lieutenant A. J. Redman, R.A.F.
Midshipman Andrew W. E. Welchman, R.N.R.

MEN.

	OFF. NO.
Ordinary Seaman William H. Allwright ...	J.62942
Officers' Cook 1st Class William Davis ...	L.5900
Ordinary Seaman R. Rawthorne.	
Petty Officer Robert H. C. Etherington.	
Able Seaman William Denning.	
Sergeant-Mechanic Quantrell, R.A.F.	
Able Seaman Denis Higgins	J.48397
Officers' Steward 3rd Class Harry Jennings ...	L.11219
Engine - Room Artificer 4th Class Francis Puckey	M.15881
Stoker Petty Officer Stanley Bowden ...	K.8442
Petty Officer William Withington ...	209115
Leading Telegraphist George A. Knight ...	J.3316
Stoker 1st Class James Holden	K.3198
Able Seaman Edward G. Robbins	J.21087
Able Seaman Frederick Bedding	J.32081
Able Seaman Harry Martin	S.S.6655
Able Seaman Samuel T. Dark	J.6562
Stoker 1st Class John R. Downes	K.1860
Officers' Steward 3rd Class Herbert Hanlon ...	L.8103
Able Seaman Stringer.	

THE ARMY.

OFFICERS.

45TH BATTALION, ROYAL FUSILIERS.

Captain F. G. Cavendish, M.C.
Lieutenant C. H. Fuller, M.C.
Lieutenant K. P. Smith.
Lieutenant G. J. Kirkcaldy.
Lieutenant H. J. Clapperton, M.C.
Lieutenant H. Q. Coles.
Lieutenant V. J. Wheeler, M.C.

46TH BATTALION, ROYAL FUSILIERS.

Lieutenant H. M. Grant, M.C.
Lieutenant C. D. Moorhead.
Lieutenant J. B. Moffatt.
2nd-Lieutenant W. S. C. Curtiss.

OTHER RANKS.

45TH BATTALION, ROYAL FUSILIERS.

129079	Sgt.	H. Heath.
131490	Pte.	T. Grange.
130775	,,	S. Hunt.
129737	,,	J. A. Dunn.
129913	Sgt.	J. Smith.
76843	Pte.	A. Davies.
130226	,,	T. Reeves.
128946	L./Cpl.	J. Hammond.
9012	Pte.	R. Golding.
131536	Sgt.	B. Granville.
130995	L./Cpl.	F. Farnsworth.
131062	Pte.	A. Jack.
180952	,,	J. E. Taylor.
129066	Sgt.	G. Sawyer.
20842	,,	V. J. Bull.
131224	L./Cpl.	C. Keenan.
129136	,,	J. Dolan.
130983	Pte.	E. H. Crutchley.
130184	,,	W. J. Cutts.
131573	,,	F. Docherty.
130158	,,	W. Little.

129072	L./Cpl.	C. E. Middleton.
130153	Pte.	J. W. Hunter.
131056	Sgt.	G. Staunton.
130866	Pte.	C. West.
129259	,,	A. Girvan.
129961	,,	J. White.
128989	L./Cpl.	S. Gale.
131144	Pte.	T. Grant.
129995	L./Cpl.	W. Wright.
129789	Pte.	W. Kennedy.
130019	C.S.M.	W. Borley.
131030	L./Cpl.	F. Eaves.
130841	Pte.	E. Gawne.
130941	Pte.	W. Lowe.
129991	Sgt.	W. Glanville.
129060	Cpl.	G. E. Coleclough.
129240	L./Cpl.	W. Whitelaw.
129075	,,	E. Lyons.
130207	Pte.	J. W. Hardy.
130186	,,	D. Bown.
129201	,,	H. Klebar.
131488	,,	T. Roach.
131216	,,	A. Hutchinson.
130845	,,	D. Judson.
101022	,,	A. II. Lane.
129006	Sgt.	L. Whitbread.
14319	Pte.	D. Capel, D.C.M.
129017	Sgt.	N. Sinnes.
129652	Pte.	F. Skidmore.
129025	,,	A. Arnott.
131018	,,	J. W. Bodman.
129002	,,	D. Murphy.
129085	,,	H. G. Morris.
291663	L./Cpl.	E. A. Roberts.
131586	Pte.	W. Wakely.
131263	,,	L. Woodcock.
128944	,,	F. Brown.
123007	,,	Purdue.
129937	,,	G. Cressy.
133025	,,	O. C. Anderson.
129640	,,	W. Ross, M.M.
130936	,,	L. Dunn.

46TH BATTALION, ROYAL FUSILIERS.

131804	Sgt.	J. McBeth.
130695	Pte.	D. Lyons.

130469	Pte.	E. Nolan.
130694	,,	W. N. Gough.
131640	,,	E. Ninno.
129887	,,	J. Park.
133213	,,	J. Adshead.
129261	,,	A. Lonsdale.
131718	Sgt.	W. Adams.
131674	Pte.	H. Spinks.
131658	,,	F. Parker.
131089	,,	A. Harvey.
129717	,,	P. Clarke.
131425	,,	W. Whiteman.
129872	,,	M. Weldon.
131345	,,	R. Clarke.
133215	,,	H. James.
131373	,,	C. Holloway.
126772	,,	J. Murphy.
130385	,,	J. Chester.
130395	L./Cpl.	C. Pettipierre.
129830	,,	J. Gallaghur.
130339	Pte.	P. Hawkins.
131181	,,	E. Collins.
131853	,,	P. Kelly.
131788	,,	S. Alcock.
129860	,,	J. Burns.
131711	,,	F. Morris.
131798	,,	J. Redmond.
130560	Sgt.	T. Goodchild.
131434	Pte.	L. Ulyatt.
130416	L./Cpl.	J. Hursey.
129499	Pte.	J. Jones.

385TH FIELD COMPANY, ROYAL ENGINEERS.

20234	Cpl.	D. Logan.

MISSING

OFFICERS.

ROYAL AIR FORCE.

Lieutenant H. L. Marshall.
Lieutenant G. Lansdowne.

OTHER RANKS.

45TH BATTALION, ROYAL FUSILIERS.

129626	Pte.	A. Sweeting.
131063	,,	J. Wynne.
128954	,,	E. J. Preston.
129662	,,	N. E. Searle.
131048	,,	J. Mack.
129956	Cpl.	A. England.
131253	Pte.	F. Swindon.
131005	,,	H. Stone.
129086	,,	P. Parker.
128982	L./Cpl.	S. W. Bray.
131264	,,	F. Hamlett.
131584	Pte.	T. Todd.

46TH BATTALION, ROYAL FUSILIERS.

131232	Sgt.	W. J. McPhee.
131363	Pte.	D. Marks.
130430	,,	H. Farlowe.
131200	,,	E. Twiner.

ROYAL ARMY MEDICAL CORPS.

200119	Pte.	J. W. Rhodes.
22005	,,	J. Ashton.
7878	,,	F. Brindle.
220044	,,	H. T. Cochrane.
12756	,,	B. Doyle.
220053	,,	G. Hopkins.
220148	,,	J. Harvey.
200244	,,	H. Wall.

HONOURS AND AWARDS

THE NAVY

BAR TO THE DISTINGUISHED SERVICE ORDER.

Lieutenant-Commander Frank Arthur Worsley, D.S.O., R.N.R.

THE DISTINGUISHED SERVICE ORDER.

Commander Hugh Beaumont Robinson, R.N.
Commander Frank George Bramble, R.N.
Lieutenant-Commander George Hoskins Irton Parker, R.N.
Lieutenant-Commander St. Andrew Oliver St. John, R.N.
Lieutenant-Commander Francis Leonard Back, R.N.
Lieutenant-Commander Arthur J. L. Murray, O.B.E., R.N.
Lieutenant-Commander Andrew Johnstone, R.N.
Engineer Lieutenant-Commander Cecil Simpson, R.N.
Lieutenant Alan Kerr McClintock Halliley, R.N.
Acting-Lieutenant Cyril Edward McLaughlin, R.N. (since killed).

BAR TO THE DISTINGUISHED SERVICE CROSS.

Lieutenant Robert Hunter McNair, D.S.C., R.N.R.
Lieutenant Ernest William King, D.S.C., R.N.R.
Chief Gunner Daniel Patrick Joseph Enright, D.S.C., R.N.

THE DISTINGUISHED SERVICE CROSS.

Lieutenant Hugh Babington, R.N. (since died).
Lieutenant George Ernest Coker, R.N.
Lieutenant Ion Whitefoord Grove White, R.N., Commanding
   H.M.S. " Cricket."
Lieutenant Ralph Petterbridge Martin, R.N.
Lieutenant Meredith Stanton Spalding, R.N.
Lieutenant Thomas Johnson Jones, R.N.
Lieutenant Edward Templeton Grayston, R.N.R., Commanding
   H.M.S. " Cicala."
Lieutenant Clive Melbourne Sergeant, R.M.L.I.

Sub-Lieutenant Basil Theodore Brewster, R.N.
Sub-Lieutenant Archibald Hugh Mafeking Dunn, R.N.
Chief Gunner David Heard Shepherd, R.N., Commanding
H.M.S. " Step Dance."
Mate Arthur Gunning Ingram, R.N.
Midshipman Andrew William Eliot Welchman, R.N.R.

BAR TO THE DISTINGUISHED SERVICE MEDAL.

Vict. C.P.O. John Patrick Canty, D.S.M., O.N. 342015.

THE DISTINGUISHED SERVICE MEDAL.

C.E.R.A. William Albert Brigden, O.N. 271661.
A.B. William George Denning, O.N. J30300.
P.O. Robert Henry Charles Etherington, O.N. J20004.
Leading Seaman George Fender, O.N. J33242.
A.B. John Jenkins, O.N. J21002.
E.R.A. 3rd Class Robert Charles Pengelly, O.N. M5254.
Leading Seaman George Frederick Tolliday, O.N. J983.
E.R.A., 2nd Class, John William Huxley, O.N. M3631.
Yeoman of Signals George William Smith, O.N. 232282.
A.B. William James Thompson, O.N. S.S. 5974.
Leading Signalman Arthur Charlton, O.N. J4467.
Leading Seaman John William Footit, O.N. 218271.
Stoker, 1st Class, James Franklin, O.N. K2915.
A.B. Albert Greenway, O.N. J21140.
Yeoman of Signals Hubert Allen Mitchell, O.N. 205057.
A.B. William James Priest, O.N. J35620.
Signalman Alexander Christie Sinton, O.N. J25874.
P.O. Dennis William Smith, O.N. J15953.
P.O. Telegraphist Frederick Simeon Stuckey, O.N. J29.
A.B. Joseph Wilson, O.N. J35012.
P.O. Henry John Wood, O.N. J5518.
Leading Signalman Arthur Ronald Worlock, O.N. J8472.

THE MERITORIOUS SERVICE MEDAL.

Signalman Charles Thomas Dean, O.N. J30568.
Signalman Douglas Leburn Simmonds, O.N. J18807.
P.O. Telegraphist William Smith, O.N. 224098.

MENTIONED IN DISPATCHES.

Engineer-Commander Francis Howard Lyon, D.S.O., R.N.
Lieutenant-Commander Quintin Bernard Preston-Thomas, R.N.

Lieutenant-Commander Henry Edward Rendall, D.S.O., R.N.
Lieutenant-Commander Victor Isaac Griffith, R.N.
Lieutenant-Commander Philip Graves Rouse, R.N.V.R.,
Lieutenant-Commander George Hoskins Irton Parker, R.N.
Lieutenant-Commander Francis Leonard Back, R.N.
Lieutenant-Commander Andrew Johnstone, R.N.
Lieutenant-Commander Kenneth Michell, D.S.C., R.N.
Engineer Lieutenant-Commander Cecil Simpson, R.N.
Lieutenant Cecil Courtenay Dickinson, D.S.O., R.N.
Lieutenant Roger Hubert Fitzherbert-Brockholes, R.N. (killed).
Lieutenant George Evelyn Paget How, R.N.
Lieutenant William Henry Fenn, R.N.
Lieutenant Leonard John Gates, R.N.R.
Lieutenant Frederick John Yuile, R.N.R.
Lieutenant Roland George Davies, R.N.V.R.
Engineer Lieutenant Frederick Arthur Hunter, R.N.R.
Captain F. R. G. Milton, M.C., R.F.A.
2nd-Lieutenant J. H. Lawrence-Archer, R.G.A.
Mate Walter Ambrose Ford, R.N.
Warrant Shipwright Daniel Wood, R.N.
Commissioned-Shipwright David James Dalyal Mackay, R.N.
Gunner William Arthur Vinnicomb, R.N.
Midshipman John Sills Charlton, R.N.R.
Midshipman Percival Baden Powell Mellows, R.N.R.
Midshipman Robert Ivor Jones, R.N.R.
Midshipman Patrick Aubrey Smith, R.N.V.R.
C.P.O. William Ernest Wright, O.N. 204383.
C.P.O. Frederick Austin, O.N. 187723.
A.B. William John Ayling, O.N. J2428.
Chief Armourer Albert Victor Brown, O.N. 343710.
A.B. Louis Thomas Burrows, O.N. J19752.
Officers' Steward, 1st Class, Herbert Channell, O.N. L5909.
A.B. Ernest Gilbert, O.N. J27880.
C.E.R.A. Edgar Graham, O.N. 270999.
C.E.R.A. Robert Henry Harding, O.N. 270325.
Signalman Harry Hickingbotham, O.N. J39986.
Pte. John George Hudson, R.M.L.I., No. Po./12946.
Leading Seaman Francis George Martin Long, O.N. J12970.
Leading Seaman Edgar Morgan, O.N. 185675.
Joiner, 3rd Class, Arthur Oliver, O.N. M8877.
Leading Seaman George Olley, O.N. J26328.
A.B. Edwin Arthur Pharaoh, O.N. J78385.
Ch. Motor Mech. John Charles Prigmore, R.N.V.R., O.N. M.B.2276.
Sergt. Ernest Randell, R.M.L.I., No. Ch./15943.
A.B. Joseph Spragg Rhind, O.N. 192011.
Shipwright, 2nd Class, William John Stubbs, O.N. 345408.
A.B. Francis Trouten, O.N. J5780.

Pte. William James Watson, R.M.L.I., No. Ch./17098.
Armourer's Crew Herbert Angus Wright, O.N. M12645.
A.B. William Albert Bridger, O.N. J37486.
Leading Stoker Charles Lewis Davies, O.N. K19600.
Shipwright, 4th Class, Monteith Cyril Dean, O.N. M34559.
A.B. Francis John Dredge, O.N. J33540.
Shipwright, 2nd Class, John Galloway, O.N. M6441.
Cpl. Percy Mills, R.F.A., No. 292929.
A.B. Robert Benjamin Pattenden, O.N. J47685.
E.R.A., 2nd Class, Reginald James Timberley, O.N. 272249.
Signalman Alfred Weston, O.N. 227149.
Signalman Ernest Lambert Gardner, O.N. J33017.
A.B. Charles Harris, O.N. S.S.6484.
A.B. Thomas Jane, O.N. J19061.
Sergt. Alfred John Knowlson, R.M.L.I., No. Po./15263.
C.E.R.A. John Arthur Lyell, O.N. M1689.
Stoker P.O. Frederick James Santillo, O.N. K3030.
P.O. Harold Gordon Walker, O.N. 213553.
A.B. Horace Weedon, O.N. J13220.
A.B. Samuel Pugh Wood, O.N. J30038.

THE ARMY

THE VICTORIA CROSS.

No. 133003 Corporal A. P. Sullivan, Australian Imperial Forces, attached 45th Battalion Royal Fusiliers.

ORDER OF ST. MICHAEL AND ST. GEORGE.
(C.M.G.)

Lieutenant-Colonel C. S. Davies, D.S.O., Leicestershire Regiment, attached 45th Battalion Royal Fusiliers.
Lieutenant-Colonel H. H. Jenkins, D.S.O., South African Infantry, attached 46th Battalion Royal Fusiliers.

PROMOTIONS.

To be Brevet Colonel.

Major and Brevet Lieutenant-Colonel L. W. de V. Sadleir Jackson, C.B., C.M.G., D.S.O., 9th Lancers.

To be Brevet Major.

Captain J. W. G. Wyld, D.S.O., M.C., Oxford and Buckinghamshire Light Infantry.

N

BAR TO THE DISTINGUISHED SERVICE ORDER.

Major A. G. Patterson, D.S.O., M.C., King's Own Scottish Borderers, attached 45th Battalion Royal Fusiliers.
Major A. E. Percival, D.S.O., M.C., the Essex Regiment, attached 46th Battalion Royal Fusiliers.
Major H. G. Harcourt, D.S.O., M.C., 201st Battalion M.G.C.

DISTINGUISHED SERVICE ORDER.

Major C. W. Burdon, Royal Artillery.
Captain F. G. Cavendish, M.C., 1st Battalion Leinster Regiment, attached 45th Battalion Royal Fusiliers.
Captain H. Heaton, M.C., 45th Battalion Royal Fusiliers.
Captain J. C. Blackburn, M.C., West Yorks Regiment, attached 46th Battalion Royal Fusiliers.
Captain A. E. Wass, M.C., 4th Hussars, attached 46th Battalion Royal Fusiliers.
Lieutenant L. L. Green, M.C., Rifle Brigade, attached 46th Battalion Royal Fusiliers.

BAR TO THE MILITARY CROSS.

Captain G. E. R. de Miremont, D.S.O., M.C., attached 46th Battalion Royal Fusiliers.
Captain W. Newbold, M.C., attached 45th Battalion Royal Fusiliers.
Captain C. C. Foulkes, M.C., attached 45th Battalion Royal Fusiliers.
Lieutenant V. J. Wheeler, M.C., attached 45th Battalion Royal Fusiliers.
Lieutenant A. C. Pearse, M.C., attached 45th Battalion Royal Fusiliers.
Lieutenant L. W. Jones, M.C., attached 45th Battalion Royal Fusiliers.
Lieutenant S. H. Walker, M.C., attached 45th Battalion Royal Fusiliers.
Lieutenant J. H. Penson, M.C., R.E., attached 45th Battalion Royal Fusiliers.
Lieutenant H. R. Oke, M.C., attached 45th Battalion Royal Fusiliers.
2nd-Lieutenant R. Ramsey, M.C., attached 45th Battalion Royal Fusiliers.
Lieutenant S. S. Harrison, M.C., 201st Battalion M.G.C.

THE MILITARY CROSS.

Captain W. Newbold, attached 45th Battalion Royal Fusiliers.

Captain C. V. Booth, attached 45th Battalion Royal Fusiliers.

Captain J. Vallance, R.A.M.C., attached 45th Battalion Royal Fusiliers.

Captain C. Featherstone, attached 46th Battalion Royal Fusiliers.

Captain and Quartermaster J. Scaife, D.C.M., attached 46th Battalion Royal Fusiliers.

Captain G. A. Webb, 201st Battalion M.G.C.

Captain J. J. Lauder, 55th Battery Royal Artillery.

Captain J. J. Magner, 156th Field Ambulance, R.A.M.C.

Lieutenant G. C. Scholfield, attached 45th Battalion Royal Fusiliers.

Lieutenant E. L. Sutro, attached 45th Battalion Royal Fusiliers.

Lieutenant C. H. Fuller, attached 45th Battalion Royal Fusiliers.

Lieutenant J. Windsor, attached 45th Battalion Royal Fusiliers.

Lieutenant V. J. Wheeler, attached 45th Battalion Royal Fusiliers.

Lieutenant N. C. W. Flint, attached 45th Battalion Royal Fusiliers.

Lieutenant F. L. Whalley, attached 45th Battalion Royal Fusiliers.

Lieutenant W. Culbert, attached 46th Battalion Royal Fusiliers.

Lieutenant C. E. Moorhead, attached 46th Battalion Royal Fusiliers.

Lieutenant A. E. Jones, attached 46th Battalion Royal Fusiliers.

Lieutenant R. H. C. Perry, attached 46th Battalion Royal Fusiliers.

Lieutenant T. S. Dumbreck, attached 46th Battalion Royal Fusiliers.

Lieutenant H. C. Platts, 385th Field Company R.E.

Lieutenant J. B. Tinker, 250th Signal Company R.E.

Lieutenant C. D. Armstrong, 201st Battalion M.G.C.

Lieutenant C. L. Snodgrass, 201st Battalion M.G.C.

2nd-Lieutenant Hon. C. A. U. Rhys, attached 45th Battalion Royal Fusiliers.

2nd-Lieutenant A. V. Saunders, attached 45th Battalion Royal Fusiliers.

2nd-Lieutenant H. Q. Coles, attached 45th Battalion Royal Fusiliers.

2nd-Lieutenant A. Matson, attached 46th Battalion Royal Fusiliers.

2nd-Lieutenant W. S. C. Curtiss, attached 46th Battalion Royal Fusiliers.

BAR TO DISTINGUISHED CONDUCT MEDAL.
130560 Sgt. T. G. Goodchild, 46th Bn. Royal Fusiliers.
602411 ,, A. E. Green, D.C.M., M.M., Royal Engineers.

DISTINGUISHED CONDUCT MEDAL.
129963 C.S.M. E. Almey, 45th Bn. Royal Fusiliers.
133001 Sgt. W. J. Robinson, 45th Bn. Royal Fusiliers.
,, W. D. Fox, 45th Bn. Royal Fusiliers.
129603 ,, C. Hunter, 45th Bn. Royal Fusiliers.
128976 ,, E. P. Petter, 45th Bn. Royal Fusiliers.
133028 Cpl. H. Gipps, 45th Bn. Royal Fusiliers.
133005 L. Cpl. A. J. Lutterburrow, 45th Bn. Royal Fusiliers.
133029 Pte. N. M. Brooke, 45th Bn. Royal Fusiliers.
129535 Pte. R. Lees, 45th Bn. Royal Fusiliers.
130228 ,, H. L. Sharp, 45th Bn. Royal Fusiliers.
129545 ,, J. P. Mason, 45th Bn. Royal Fusiliers.
129644 ,, J. McGarry, 45th Bn. Royal Fusiliers.
14319 ,, D. Capel, 45th Bn. Royal Fusiliers.
130133 ,, J. W. Hunter, 45th Bn. Royal Fusiliers.
133039 ,, W. F. Quarrell, 45th Bn. Royal Fusiliers.
133007 ,, J. Purdue, 45th Bn. Royal Fusiliers.
130825 Sgt. R. H. F. Gascoigne-Roy, 46th Bn. Royal Fusiliers.
129518 ,, J. Whammond, M.C., 46th Bn. Royal Fusiliers.
131232 ,, W. Gale, 46th Bn. Royal Fusiliers.
129407 ,, G. H. Templeman, 46th Bn. Royal Fusiliers.
129059 Cpl. A. W. Card, 46th Royal Fusiliers.
192194 ,, G. Murphy, 201st M.G.C.
43159 ,, C. Kilby, 201st M.G.C.
345042 Sgt. J. Edmunds, M.M., 55th Battery R.F.A.

BAR TO THE MILITARY MEDAL.
133054 Cpl. H. J. M. Spies, M.M., 45th Bn. Royal Fusiliers.
129640 Pte. W. Ross, M.M., 45th Bn. Royal Fusiliers.
128963 ,, W. Wright, M.M., 45th Bn. Royal Fusiliers.
130074 ,, F. Daley, M.M., 45th Bn. Royal Fusiliers.
128903 ,, H. Taylor, M.M., 45th Bn. Royal Fusiliers.
,, J. Jones, M.M., 45th Bn. Royal Fusiliers.
129964 Sgt. T. Socket, M.M., 46th Bn. Royal Fus.
129110 Cpl. J. Johns, D.C.M., M.M., 46th Bn. Royal Fus.
131484 Pte. J. M. Ulyatt, M.M.
53580 Sgt. S. Stephenson, M.M., 201st Bn. M.G.C.
192209 Pte. P. Smith, M.M., 201st Bn. M.G.C.
198013 ,, W. Jones, M.M., 201st Bn. M.G.C.
19393 L./Cpl. A. E. McKenzie, M.M., Royal Engineers.
17863 Pte. J. Bradshaw, M.M., 155th Field Ambulance, R.A.M.C.

THE MILITARY MEDAL.

129908	C.Q.M.S.	H. Hardisty, 45th Bn. Royal Fusiliers.
130038	Sgt.	F. Durrant, 45th Bn. Royal Fusiliers.
129142	,,	W. Allington, 45th Bn. Royal Fusiliers.
129230	,,	W. Baulker, 45th Bn. Royal Fusiliers.
133063	,,	J. Roche, 45th Bn. Royal Fusiliers.
129699	Cpl.	A. Burns, 45th Bn. Royal Fusiliers.
129376	,,	C. W. McKay, 45th Bn. Royal Fusiliers.
130026	,,	W. J. H. Green, 45th Bn. Royal Fusiliers.
133092	,,	F. Wickens, 45th Bn. Royal Fusiliers.
130030	,,	J. M. Edwards, 45th Bn. Royal Fusiliers.
128960	,,	E. R. Nash, 45th Bn. Royal Fusiliers.
129927	L./Cpl.	D. Allen, D.C.M., 45th Bn. Royal Fusiliers.
130323	,,	W. Wilson, 45th Bn. Royal Fusiliers.
129181	,,	G. Baker, M.C., 45th Bn. Royal Fusiliers.
129157	,,	J. E. Holloway, 45th Bn. Royal Fusiliers.
	,,	S. Cale, 45th Bn. Royal Fusiliers.
133018	,,	J. Collins, 45th Bn. Royal Fusiliers.
131297	,,	L. P. Mordant, 45th Bb. Royal Fusiliers.
133151	Pte.	M. Butler, 45th Bn. Royal Fusiliers.
133024	,,	W. Hodson, 45th Bn. Royal Fusiliers.
131580	,,	A. McKenzie, 45th Bn. Royal Fusiliers.
130795	,,	L. F. Gooding, 45th Bn. Royal Fusiliers.
130856	,,	E. Tappin, 45th Bn. Royal Fusiliers.
200123	,,	E. Newell, R.A.M.C., attached 45th Bn. Royal Fusiliers.
131029	,,	P. Hunt, 45th Bn. Royal Fusiliers.
6430	,,	A. N. Cherrett, 45th Bn. Royal Fusiliers.
129120	,,	G. Eaton, 45th Bn. Royal Fusiliers.
129082	,,	R. McNiven, 45th Bn. Royal Fusiliers.
130120	,,	R. Sheppard, 45th Bn. Royal Fusiliers.
128950	Sgt.	A. Jones, 46th Bn. Royal Fusiliers.
129130	,,	P. Moran, D.C.M., 46th Bn. Royal Fusiliers.
130319	,,	P. Hanlon, 46th Bn. Royal Fusiliers.
130679	,,	G. Brown, 46th Bn. Royal Fusiliers.
229318	,,	J. Whammond, M.C., D.C.M., 46th Bn. Royal Fusiliers.
L/20589	,,	V. Gerhardi, 46th Bn. Royal Fusiliers.
131898	Cpl.	A. McRae, 46th Bn. Royal Fusiliers.
129308	L./Cpl.	W. A. Cannell, 46th Bn. Royal Fusiliers.
131715	,,	C. Jerram, 46th Bn. Royal Fusiliers.
130416	,,	J. Horsley, 46th Bn. Royal Fusiliers.
133338	,,	G. Little, 46th Bn. Royal Fusiliers.
133288	,,	J. Brogan, 46th Bn. Royal Fusiliers.
129776	Pte.	C. Ferguson, 46th Bn. Royal Fusiliers.
131675	,,	P. Mack, 46th Bn. Royal Fusiliers.

129429	Pte.	E. C. Marriott, 46th Bn. Royal Fusiliers.
131303	,,	J. W. Purvis, 46th Bn. Royal Fusiliers.
131623	,,	H. McPherson, 46th Bn. Royal Fusiliers.
130641	,,	C. Donovan, 46th Bn. Royal Fusiliers.
130440	,,	W. Perkins, 46th Bn. Royal Fusiliers.
130433	,,	J. Reilly, 46th Bn. Royal Fusiliers.
131829	,,	M. Fearon, 46th Bn. Royal Fusiliers.
129737	.,	S. Yeardley, 46th Bn. Royal Fusiliers.
131074	,,	G. Went, 46th Bn. Royal Fusiliers.
181853	,,	F. Kelly, 46th Bn. Royal Fusiliers.
130423	,,	H. Jamieson, 46th Bn. Royal Fusiliers.
131084	,,	A. Davis, 46th Bn. Royal Fusiliers.
9788	Far. S./Sgt.	J. Druce, 250th Signal Company, R.E.
24750	Spr.	R. H. Collyer, 250th Signal Company, R.E.
24991	,.	H. Tomlinson, 250th Signal Company, R.E.
25839	,,	C. Milford, 250th Signal Company, R.E.
344031	,,	J. C. Pope, 250th Signal Company, R.E.
197119	,,	R. H. Graham, 250th Signal Company, R.E.
253382	Dvr.	C. W. Keane, 250th Signal Company, R.E.
602439	Pioneer	G. Wheatley, 250th Signal Company, R.E.
602427	,,	F. G. Mansfield, 250th Signal Company, R.E.
113936	L./Cpl.	R. Parry, 201st Bn. M.G.C.
1014	Cpl.	A. L. Morton, 201st Bn. M.G.C.
1797	Gdsm.	J. Hubbard, 201st Bn. M.G.C.
70922	Pte.	J. Hilston, 201st Bn. M.G.C.
7887	Gdsm.	A. Dove, 201st Bn. M.G.C.
15111	Sgt.	W. A. Clements, 55th Battery R.F.A.
39119	Bdr.	G. F. Marshall, 55th Battery R.F.A.
128824	Sgt.	P. V. Morrish, 385th Field Company R.E.
602521	2/Cpl.	D. M. Hogge, Royal Engineers.
25381	Spr.	F. Iveson, Royal Engineers.
602743	,,	T. G. Paul, Royal Engineers.
328829	,,	G. W. Leitch, Royal Engineers.
144790	,,	P. Cross, Royal Engineers.
344852	,,	J. Chinnery, 385th Field Company, R.E.
344071	Dvr.	C. H. Page, 385th Field Company, R.E.
18418	S./Sgt.	G. Smith, 155th Field Ambulance.
1859	Pte.	W. R. Green, Royal Army Medical Corps.
180978	,,	J. R. Allon, 155th Field Ambulance, R.A.M.C.
220000	,,	H. J. Sprigge, 155th Field Ambulance, R.A.M.C
220099	,,	G. E. Honeywill, 155th Field Ambulance, R.A.M.C.
220044	,,	H. T. Cochrane, 155th Field Ambulance, R.A.M.C.
94298	,,	G. Gibbons, 155th Field Ambulance, R.A.M.C.

MERITORIOUS SERVICE MEDAL.

192107	Sgt.	W. Brassey, 201st Bn. M.G.C.
28750	,,	W. P. Warnock, 1st Oxford and Bucks L.I.
21253	,,	E. A. Manning, R.A.S.C.
64027	Cpl.	W. Baddams, 1st Oxford and Bucks L.I.
39974	,,	L. Nock, 1st Oxford and Bucks L.I.
	,,	H. W. Hammersley, 46th Bn. Royal Fusiliers.
	,,	T. W. Minksley, 45th Bn. Royal Fusiliers.

MENTIONED IN DISPATCHES.

BRIGADE HEADQUARTERS.

Lieutenant-Colonel E. M. Browne, C.M.G., Royal Engineers.
Captain J. H. Pickering, The Gloucester Regiment.
Captain S. R. W. Benedick, The Yorkshire Regiment.
Captain G. Darby, Royal Artillery.
Lieutenant C. N. Brownhill, Royal Artillery.

45TH BN. ROYAL FUSILIERS.

R.Q.M.S. T. W. Brown.
C.S.M. A. Bishork, M.M.

46TH BN. ROYAL FUSILIERS.

Captain C. R. Williams, D.S.O., M.C.
Major C. G. W. Nightingale, M.C.
Lieutenant E. V. Burke-Murphy, M.C.
Lieutenant W. E. Gage.
Lieutenant C. Lloyd.
Lieutenant T. C. Clarke.
2nd-Lieutenant A. Smith, D.C.M., M.M.
C.S.M. W. W. Wodehouse.
C.S.M. C. Hardy.
C.S.M. R. Porter.
Cpl. P. Alexander.
L./Sgt. W. Gale.
C.Q.M.S. A. G. Nichol.
Sgt. J. Whammond, M.C., D.C.M., M.M.
Cpl. A. N. Smith.
Pte. H. Whittington.
Pte. P. Donnelly.

201st Battn. Machine Gun Corps.

Lieutenant P. D. Morrison.
R.Q.M.S. G. F. Bennett.
Sgt. R. Wilkinson.
C.Q.M.S. Setford.
Sgt. M. A. MacCorkindale.
Cpl. W. Scott.

Royal Field Artillery.

Captain M. D. Motion.
Lieutenant J. J. Lauder.

250th Signal Company, R.E.

Cpl. H. Perkin.
Sgt. T. Stannard.
Sgt. R. Fletcher.
Spr. F. G. Prior.

385th Field Company, R.E.

Captain W. G. Pearson.
Lieutenant H. K. Armytage.
2nd-Lieutenant A. L. Green.
T./C.S.M. L. Harvey.
Spr. W. J. Smith.
Spr. A. G. Lamb.

155th Field Ambulance.

Pte. W. Moore.
Sgt. J. Percy, D.C.M.
Sgt. R. Kearns, M.M.
Q.M.S. D. Parker.
Pte. W. Campbell.

R.A.S.C.

C.S.M. L. Makin.
S./Sgt. F. C. R. Pettyfer.
Sgt. R. Perry.

Interpreters.

A./Sgt. G. Edgar.
Sgt. J. Godfrey.

Vaga Column.

Lieutenant H. Gibbons.
Lieutenant W. L. Dibben, M.C.
Private W. Sparks.

RUSSIAN AWARDS

ORDER OF ST. GEORGE, FOURTH CLASS.

Brigadier-General L. W. de V. Sadleir-Jackson, C.B., C.M.G.. D.S.O.

SAINT ANNA, SECOND CLASS WITH SWORDS AND RIBAND.

Lieutenant-Colonel C. M. Browne, C.M.G., D.S.O., R.E.
Lieutenant-Colonel C. S. Davies, D.S.O., 45th Bn. Royal Fusiliers.
Lieutenant-Colonel H. H. Jenkins, D.S.O., 46th Bn. Royal Fusiliers.
Lieutenant-Colonel H. Pritchard-Taylor, D.S.O., M.C., R.A.M.C.
Lieutenant-Colonel T. E. Harty, D.S.O., R.A.M.C.
Lieutenant-Colonel Tomkinson, R.A.F.
Lieutenant-Colonel E. C. T. Minet, D.S.O., M.C., M.G.C.

SAINT ANNA, THIRD CLASS WITH SWORDS AND RIBAND.

Major G. H. Cammell, R.F.A.
Captain G. P. Simpson, R.F.A.
Captain W. B. Wishaw, R.E.
Captain J. W. G. Wyld, D.S.O., M.C., Oxford and Bucks L.I.
Captain G. R. Prendergast, 46th Bn. Royal Fusiliers.
Captain J. C. Blackburn, 46th Bn. Royal Fusiliers.
Major H. N. G. Watson, D.S.O., R.A.S.C.
Captain W. J. Knight, M.C., R.A.M.C.
Lieutenant C. N. Brownhill, M.C., R.F.A.
Lieutenant C. L. Snodgrass, 201st Bn. M.G.C.

SAINT STANISLAS, SECOND CLASS WITH SWORDS.

Major C. W. Burdon, R.F.A.
Major R. Luby, D.S.O., M.C., R.E.
Major H. G. Harcourt, D.S.O., M.C., 201st Bn. M.G.C.
Captain (Brevet Major) A. G. Paterson, M.C., K.O.S.B. (attached 45th Bn. Royal Fusiliers).

SAINT STANISLAS, THIRD CLASS WITH SWORDS.

Lieutenant J. C. Zigomala, Irish Guards.
Lieutenant A. Whalley, 45th Bn. Royal Fusiliers.
Lieutenant W. Wheeler, 45th Bn. Royal Fusiliers.

CROIX SAINT GEORGES.

129068	Sgt.	Howard, 45th Bn. Royal Fusiliers.
130307	Pte.	Jenkins, 45th Bn. Royal Fusiliers.
131747	,,	Pond, 46th Bn. Royal Fusiliers.
131883	,,	Wilson, 46th Bn. Royal Fusiliers.
62536	Cpl.	G. Easton, R.F.A.
45964	Gnr.	R. G. Miles, R.G.A.
3149	S./Sgt.	E. A. Carter, R.E. (Engineer Clerk).
ES/50646	T./Cpl.	S. G. Staff, R.A.S.C.
155650	Cpl.	H. E. Digby, R.A.M.C.

MEDAILLE SAINT GEORGES.

130213	C.S.M.	Bowen, 46th Bn. Royal Fusiliers.
131086	Pte.	S. Morrison, 46th Bn. Royal Fusiliers.
129155	Cpl.	Litkie, 45th Bn. Royal Fusiliers.
131576	Pte.	Bollanger, 45th Bn. Royal Fusiliers.
25496	Sgt.	T. Parks, R.F.A.
23215	Gnr.	R. Gloin, R.F.A.
37623	Bdr.	F. Fairweather, R.F.A.
602456	Spr.	H. J. Rose, R.E.
602424	Sgt.	W. Hawkins, R.E.
2887	Spr.	A. Nimmo, R.E.
192110	Sgt.	C. Oliver, 201st Bn. M.G.C.
86986	Cpl.	C. Brown, 201st Bn. M.G.C.
192222	Pte.	E. S. Strangen, 201st Bn. M.G.C.
192228	,,	A. H. Bennett, 201st Bn. M.G.C.
67959	,,	W. C. Freshwater, 201st Bn. M.G.C.

www.ingramcontent.com/pod-product-compliance
Lightning Source LLC
Chambersburg PA
CBHW030404100426
42812CB00028B/2832/J